Partnering for Profit

Success Strategies for Tomorrow's Supply Chain

SUSAN PHILLIPS BARI

Published by the Women's Business Enterprise National Council (WBENC)
1120 Connecticut Avenue, NW
Suite 1000
Washington DC, 20036

Cover Design by n8 Solutions
Text Design by Budget Book Design

First Edition: June 2005

Please visit www.WBENC.org for more information about WBENC or to order additional copies of this book. WBENC offers special quantity discounts for bulk purchase. Excerpts of this book may be used with written consent from WBENC.

Library of Congress Control Number: 2005923894

ISBN: 0-9753928-1-6

Printed in the United States of America
Published in Washington, DC

Dedication

This book is dedicated to the leadership of the Women's Business Enterprise National Council, who have guided its growth and success since its inception in 1997.

Deborah Cannon,
NationsBank – Acting Chair – 1997

William J. Alcorn,
JC Penney Company,
Chair of the Board, 1997 - 2000

Enid Winn,
JPMorgan Chase, 2000 - 2002

Joan Kerr,
SBC Communications, 2002 -2005

Acknowledgements

I have always been an advocate of collaboration. This book, whose topic is alliances, could not have been completed without the partnerships of many people who have been involved with bringing it from concept to your eyes.

The book's editor is Ginger Conrad, known to all of you as the founder and publisher of *MBE Magazine*. Ginger generously devoted an enormous amount of time to making certain that the book was consistent and accurate. Her experience and knowledge of both facts and people have been invaluable. I could not have done it without her and she has my eternal gratitude.

My enormously capable collaborator again is Lindsey Pollak. Lindsey is a book "coach," who keeps the book writing process on schedule, conducts research and interviews and pulls together both concepts and edits. For all of you who have ever said "I want to write a book someday," Lindsey can help you bring that dream to reality.

Danielle Walton, WBENC's Program Manager and editor of my monthly e-newsletter ,*President's Report*, played the important role of "publisher," coordinating designers, printers and all of the other logistical details necessary to keeping a publication date on track. Danielle's mother is a published author and I believe that someday she will be as well.

I thank all of our corporate members who have added comments and success stories to these pages, the leadership of our 14 regional partner organizations, and our certified women business enterprises for providing their invaluable expertise and stories of partnerships. You can read more about many of them in this book's Appendices.

Finally, I want to thank Kathy Greco of Manpower, who believed in and supported the concept of *Partnering for Profit* before I had put pen to paper. Manpower provided a grant that enabled the work on the book to progress and to make it available free of charge to all attendees of Women in Business 2005, WBENC's national conference and business fair. Thank you, Kathy, for your vision and for supporting WBENC's vision.

Not least of all, I thank you, the reader, who will work to form the alliances and success stories that will drive our mission—to create success for our corporate members and certified women's business enterprises in partnership with our regional affiliate organizations.

CONTENTS

Foreword

When Manpower pioneered the staffing industry in the 1940s, the company's success depended on the very same thing it does today now that we have grown to be a world leader in the business: our ability to make the best match between job candidate and employer.

This focus gives us a profound appreciation for Susan Phillips Bari and her leadership of the Women's Business Enterprise National Council (WBENC). After all, the success of WBENC and its members also weighs on making the right match—the match between women's business enterprises and corporations.

Although it has been less than a decade since Susan founded WBENC, she and the organization have already left a legacy on the women's business community. WBENC not only serves as a unified voice and catalyst for opportunity for woman-owned businesses across the country, but it also provides a certification process that sets the standard for quality among U.S. businesses owned and operated by women.

For these reasons, women business owners have cause to celebrate each time they catch a glimpse of Susan's business savvy. That said, a champagne toast is in order for *Partnering for Profit.*

This one-stop guide is not just about tapping into the corporate supply chain. Rather, it's about knowing how to build relationships that showcase your impact on the value corporations bring to their customers. As a corporate member of WBENC, Manpower knows this value firsthand from the many women's business enterprises that have helped us build one of the most enviable—and profitable—supplier diversity programs in the staffing industry.

My perspective on the important role of women in business has deepened since I became the leader of Manpower's North American organization. It is easy to see why when you consider that three quarters of Manpower's U.S. managers are women with profit and loss responsibility.

I am fortunate to be part of a company with a foundation that was built on women's advancement. Even with this foundation, however, Manpower has relied on WBENC to help us ensure that women are as much an organic part of our supply chain as they are inside the walls of our company.

The two dynamics do not always occur naturally, nor do they necessarily go hand-in-hand, underscoring the importance of the insight Susan shares in *Partnering for Profit*. There are many factors to consider as you prepare to partner with corporations in a way that makes you indispensable to the supply chain.

The good news is that the marketplace is rich with opportunities for you to build corporate relationships that will boost the bottom line for you, for them and for customers. Even better news is that the steps to help you get started are neatly outlined in these pages. You will be motivated by the success stories of those who are already partnering for profit, and you will identify tactics you can adopt in your own approach.

I wish you the best in growing your business, and I am confident that, after reading the compelling advice Susan shares in this book, your efforts to partner for profit will be met with great success.

Barbara J. Beck
Executive Vice President, U.S. & Canadian Operations
Manpower Inc.

Introduction

Immediately after I finished writing my first book, *Breaking Through: Creating Opportunities for America's Women and Minority Owned Businesses,* I knew that my next project had to be a book about partnerships and alliances. It is impossible to talk about success in business—or in life, for that matter—without addressing the crucial importance of relationships. Just as the old Gaelic proverb says (although not in a politically correct manner!), "A man is known by the company he keeps." Given today's corporate emphasis on supply chain management and effectiveness, partnering is not just a good idea, but absolutely mandatory. Of the numerous trends impacting corporate purchasing and diversity efforts today, the push to cut costs, the impact of bundled contracts and the trend toward centralization in purchasing within organizations are having the most significant impact on large corporations and, ultimately, on women business enterprises' access to markets.

The idea of writing a book on partnering had been building in my mind for a while. About four years ago I attended a meeting of the Billion Dollar Roundtable. The Roundtable was created by diversity publisher Don McKneely (*Minority Business News USA* and *WE, Inc.* magazines) to recognize the accomplishments and capture the best practices of companies whose diversity spend exceeds $1 billion per year. Ten corporations were inducted that first year and others have been added since that time, a reflection of the growing recognition at the highest levels of corporate America that supply chains must mirror the demographic makeup of customers and communities. I was invited to attend and participate in the meetings surrounding the recognition event as a representative of women's business enterprises.

JUST-IN-TIME LEARNING:
The Billion Dollar Roundtable

The Billion Dollar Roundtable (BDR) refers to companies that spend over $1 billion with Growth Market Enterprise (GME) suppliers. As of March, 2005, members of the BDR, in alphabetical order, include:

- Altria
- AT&T
- DaimlerChrysler
- Ford Motor Company
- General Motors
- IBM
- Johnson Controls
- Lockheed Martin
- Lucent Technologies
- SBC Communications
- Verizon Communications
- Wal-Mart Stores

Ford Motor Company received the top honor that first year and one of its senior executives provided interesting and forward-looking remarks. After he thanked the Roundtable for the recognition, he cautioned that the $3.2 billion spent the prior year included spending with only about 300 companies. He promised that the dollar value of the contracts would not be decreased, but advised that the number of suppliers could be. Ford, like other automakers, is reducing the size of its supply base and diverse suppliers are not immune from the economics of the marketplace. He advised woman- and minority-owned businesses that they needed to put their CEO egos aside and take a page from the book of the large corporations that were merging to create economies of scale and increased profitability for their shareholders.

This comment led to my first of two "light bulb" moments at that event.

I knew I had to pay close attention as president of an organization dedicated to providing our corporate members with certified woman-owned businesses, and to furthering opportunities for women business owners in their supply chains. Corporations, thanks to the major changes in business technology at the end of the twentieth century, have become able to more closely monitor their own cost of doing business and to drill down and analyze the cost of each check issued or invoice received. In their drive to improve processes and become more profitable, they began, among other process improvements, to compress their supply chains. This, in turn, meant that opportunities for smaller companies would be pushed down to second tier or even third tier.

At the time, I was quite familiar with a similar term from the government sector, "contract bundling." Whatever you called this practice, I understood that the compression of the supply chain was a growing challenge that Growth Market Enterprises (or GMEs – my preferred term for all diversity businesses) would face as they tried to compete for corporate contracts. I knew that the Women's Business Enterprise National Council (WBENC) would have to respond to what I saw as a challenge for the future place of GMEs in America's corporate supply chain. As WBENC is a corporate membership organization, we owed it to our corporate partners to assist them with their goal of maintaining and growing a diverse supply base while also meeting the mandates of efficiency within their organizations. Prior to my experience at the Billion Dollar Roundtable event, I had most often seen the issue of supply chain compression and bundling addressed at technology-related workshops, seminars and presentations for women business enterprises (WBEs), including our own B2B Survival Training funded by the PepsiCo Foundation. After my Billion Dollar Roundtable experience, I began to understand that the issue was far more complex and involved much more than technology integration concerns.

I determined that WBENC's response would not be to change our focus or mission, but to add programs and provide products that would assist both our corporate members and certified WBEs to develop and maintain a competitive edge. One of the new products we provided our corporate members was a balanced score card (see Appendix A) that provides the opportunity to measure the cost savings to the corporation for its WBE spend, thus assisting them in making the diversity business case within their companies.

My second light bulb moment at the Roundtable concerned how WBENC could help certified WBEs adapt to changes in the marketplace—to keep pace with the goals of their corporate customers. Early in the 1990s I founded and ran a women's business training center and we frequently came across and worked with various business "incubators" that assisted start-up companies with infrastructure support. They sometimes provided shared office space, copiers and fax machines and some provided counseling on basic business issues such as record keeping, insurance and marketing. What I realized that day at the Roundtable was that the businesses certified by WBENC and the National Minority Supplier Development Council (NMSDC) are beyond the need for an incubator, but given the new business landscape, they could certainly use an "accelerator." I thought that no time should be wasted in figuring out what resources were available to each individual supplier and how those resources could be maximized to rapidly spur growth. I began to plan programs, events and, of course, books. As you will see on the pages of this book, partnering is an important strategy for

GME businesses' acceleration.

Partnering for Profit: Success Strategies for Tomorrow's Supply Chain is but one of the tools that WBENC is honing to assist our WBEs and other GMEs as they face the challenges of today's supply chain environment—to accelerate them at the same speed as corporate America. In turn, their increased capacity and supply chain sophistication will provide increased resources for corporations to continue to pursue the efficiencies of supply chain management with diverse suppliers maintaining a role as prime suppliers.

In what other ways has WBENC helped WBEs accelerate and keep pace with their corporate customers thus far? The Tuck/WBENC Executive Management Program, underwritten by IBM and launched in 2003, prepares women to move from entrepreneur to CEO as their business grows. The education provided by the Dartmouth College Tuck School of Business faculty enables women leaders to develop the same level of expertise as the corporate executives with whom they interact. (Tuck also provides two similar programs for minority entrepreneurs and has built a reputation for excellence in this arena for more than 25 years.) WBENC's annual *Women in Business: Sharing the Vision* conference and business fair held every June provides a platform for interaction and an opportunity for corporations and WBEs alike to showcase their capabilities. Cutting-edge workshops designed and executed by our corporate members, experienced WBEs and executives from our partner organizations bring these issues to the front burner and provide information, follow-on resources and take-away tools to further the continued partnership between corporate procurement programs and WBE suppliers. My first book, *Breaking Through,* provides a history of supplier diversity and examines successful strategies for marketing. I encourage all WBEs to take advantage of these various resources, if you have not already.

Partnering for Profit: Success Strategies for Tomorrow's Supply

Chain is the next step in the business acceleration process. I believe that today's WBEs must form alliances, partnerships and joint ventures in order to remain competitive in the new world of shrinking corporate supply chains. I also challenge corporations to consider procedures for encouraging partnerships between women and minority owned companies. Corporate members have extended the first hand by partnering with WBENC to examine supply chain issues in our Strategic Sourcing and Supply Chain Effectiveness Board committee and by sponsoring and participating in national conferences and regional procurement programs conducted by our women's business organization partners throughout the United States.

While partnering is a very serious business for GMEs, creating alliances is not necessarily difficult. This book will provide critical information about increasing profitability for both GMEs and their corporate and government customers, and we will try to do it in a manner that is user-friendly. I hope my male readers will excuse the format that provides analogies that every woman understands: dating, courtship and marriage. Throughout this book I will often refer to the parallels between these romantic relationships and business relationships. I find it quite instructive (and amusing!) to bring out the similarities. As all married people know, relationships take a lot of work, but the rewards are immeasurable. The advice we have been seeking, reading and sharing all of our lives to make our personal relationships work can also make our business relationships work.

In forging any relationship—new, old, personal, professional—you have to put aside all of your assumptions and start with a clean slate and an open mind...and a great plan, which is what I hope you will take away when you finish this book. On the following pages you will enjoy access to the tips, tricks and to-dos of many corporate and entrepreneurial experts who have been generous enough to share their advice with you. As with

Breaking Through, the advice is particularly targeted to the unique needs of and opportunities available to certified women and minority business owners, but is certainly applicable to "majority" business as well.

Keep in mind as you read every page of this book that your partnerships must be a "win-win-win." A win for you, a win for your partners (whether they are bound to you in formal and permanent relationships or just on board for a project or period of time) and a third win for your corporate clients that will benefit from the accelerated capacity your company has to offer their supply chain.

I also urge you to pay particular attention to the "Profitable Partnerships" profiles in each chapter. These are real stories, positive and negative, of real partnerships. My goal in sharing these stories is to help you avoid reinventing the partnership wheel with each new relationship, and also to help you avoid some common mistakes. I also hope that you will share *Partnering for Profit* with your current and future business partners. Just like the tools and strategies presented in a marriage advice book, this information is most helpful when it is applied by both parties!

I wish you the best of luck with all of your partnerships, both personal and professional.

Susan Phillips Bari
February 2005
Washington, DC

Chapter One:

The Building Blocks of Partnership

Before we get started, answer this question: Do you want more business than you have today? If the answer is "no," feel free to close this book right now and head off to the beach. If you do want more business—and I think we all do!—then take a moment to think about why you are not getting it. It is my deep belief that partners are essential to any and all business growth. In today's competitive, fast-paced business world, with the challenges of constant technology changes and compressed supply chains, you simply

cannot go it alone. I could not move WBENC forward if it were not for the support I get from my #1 partner—my husband Dick. I say this not to win points (with him or with you), but to point out at the outset that we find and need partners in many areas of our businesses and our lives to become and remain successful. Your "partner's" name might not be on the office door and the relationship might not be formalized in a contract or in articles of incorporation, but they contribute to your success nonetheless.

FAST FACTS

Forty-five percent of certified Women Business Enterprises report that they have formed a joint venture or strategic alliance to bid on an opportunity with a large corporation.
- "Access to Markets: Perspectives from Large Corporations and Women's Business Enterprises" conducted by Center for Women's Business Research and commissioned by WBENC, Women Entrepreneurs' Connection at FleetBoston Financial and the Ewing Marion Kauffman Foundation, 2003.

You will note throughout the book that I employ a very broad definition of the term "partner." Without a doubt you as a business owner already have many partners, even more than you may realize. This is why I stated in the Introduction that partnership is a serious endeavor, but not necessarily a difficult one. You just have to start by increasing your awareness and the way you view the people and companies that make up your company's network and environment. Partners include, but are not limited to: your funders (including the provider of your line of credit, family members who helped you with start-up costs and provided ongoing support, and maybe even your credit card company); your diversity certification organization, your suppliers who provide you with quality products and services, your employees, your interns, your babysitter and, of course, your clients or customers. Do not ever forget that your primary customers are also your partners and need to be treated as active partners in your growth. Also, whether you are an entrepreneur or in a corporate position, do not discount the important support role played by members of your family. If you look at partnership with this very inclusive definition, developing new partnerships should not be a scary prospect at all.

PROFITABLE PARTNERSHIP:
Management Alternatives

Patricia Henriquez was the office manager for a big Washington, DC law firm. The company was challenged with a major "renovation in place" that required that all or some of the firm had to relocate every six weeks for 18 months. "We could only do little pieces at a time," Pat recalls. "It was quite a challenge to keep systems working and attorneys productive and happy."

At the completion of the job, both the general contractor and the interior designer approached Pat and suggested she start a company. Pat liked the idea, but having had no experience as a CEO, she was a little concerned: not about her ability to manage services and work with contractors, designers and real estate firms, but about the things she did not know, such as business planning and marketing.

From the outset, Pat recruited a paid board of directors to "fill in the gaps" in her knowledge base and keep the new company on a productive track. With her board, Pat wrote a business plan and marketing study and in July 1983, launched Management Alternatives (MA). The company began with a host of administrative services to augment the relocation specialty and took as one of its first clients a group of attorneys from the old firm that had set up shop. Pat employed an innovative marketing strategy that relied on informal partnerships. "We knew we did not have enough money for a large sales force and had to figure out how to get information to the end user on what was basically a new service."

The first breakthrough moment came when MA attained its first major client: General Electric. The business opportunity came from a referral from another client. As a matter of fact, most of MA's business came from contractor and interior designer referrals. Other "partners" on the real estate team could see a benefit to their client by having MA on the team. Pat explains, "We were not a subcontractor, nor did we have an official alliance agreement. They referred us as an outside service that the client should consider as part of the relocation or renovation. Later, when we did larger projects, we were brought on as a team member and our costs were included in the bid. They were our sales people. We did presentations to them and they made the pitches to their clients. Business-to-business marketing would have been much more difficult without these introductions."

This informal partnership among various suppliers in this particular supply chain was truly a "win-win-win" situation, a term you will hear much more about later in this chapter. The general contractors, real estate companies and interior designers understood the value proposition. The last thing the client remembered was the move, and if that went smoothly, they had a good feeling about the entire project. If the move was a nightmare, everyone shared the pain. The client benefited from a smooth transition with the least possible disturbance to their business processes.

The Innovative Partnership Model of WBENC

WBENC itself was founded on the theory that a wide net of partners would be needed to accomplish our mission: to increase opportunities in the business marketplace for companies owned and run by women. Our initial partnership model is the same today—comprising corporations with supplier diversity programs, certified women-owned businesses and regional women's business organizations. To date, our original list of 11 partner corporations has grown to 200, our four women's business organization partners to 14, and fewer than 500 certified businesses to more than 5,000. Each new partner adds value to our basic goal: increasing opportunities for success for all of our partners.

According to Julie White of McKinley Marketing Partners, who prepared our 2003 branding study, WBENC's partnership model is highly unique and "a model for the future." Why? At WBENC we consciously bring people around the table who are usually across the table from each other.

For instance, women business owners and corporate supplier diversity professionals are often on opposite sides of the negotiating table, but we engage them in a relationship-building dialogue to help determine the direction of various WBENC initiatives. In addition to the many corporations in a diverse range of industries who populate our Board of Directors and national and regional committees, we also bring together various women's organizations (most importantly our affiliated Women's Business Organization Partners, or WBOPs, which are key to our growth potential and success), minority business organizations, Chambers of Commerce and others to discuss joint programs to benefit our various constituencies. We have formal Memoranda of Understanding with some, like the United States Hispanic Chamber of Commerce, the National Association of Women in Construction and Quantum Leaps, Inc., and work in more informal ways with others, like the National Association of Women Business Owners (NAWBO). We believe that partnership is about respecting everyone you work with and building mutual respect, support and success.

The top organizations in the country that advocate on behalf of women in business collaborate frequently, share information, speak at one another's programs, and even serve on one another's boards and advisory councils. For example, WBENC is an organizational partner of Women Impacting Public Policy (WIPP) and recently agreed to head up its strategic alliances council. I serve on their advisory board and our Women's Enterprise Leadership Forum relies on WIPP's information on government contracting issues as well as public policy debate and development on issues that affect all small businesses, such as health care costs, prison labor, taxes and business regulatory issues. Frequently, WIPP provides opportunities for WBEs to testify before Congress, participate in Roundtables and even meet with the President of the United States and his key policy aides. Interestingly, WIPP itself was formed as a strategic alliance. Rather than going out and only focusing on recruiting women business owners, WIPP's founders Terry Neese and Barbara Kasoff used their many years of advocacy in the women's business community to reach out to other organizations whose members then become part of their network.

"NONPROFIT-ABLE" PARTNERSHIP: Women Impacting Public Policy

Terry Neese and Barbara Kasoff are co-founders of Women Impacting Public Policy (WIPP), a national bi-partisan public policy organization representing more than 505,000 women in business and women business owners nationwide. How do these women from opposite sides of the aisle make their partnership work for a diverse membership? They believe in partnering on many levels.

"It was incredible to us that in the year 2001, there was no organized effort to bring women, and especially women in business, together in a united voice to advocate on legislative issues important to women in business, nor was there an effort to ensure we had a 'seat at the table' of economic power or political power," Terry says. "We believed a bi-partisan effort was not only necessary but a must! We believed we could accomplish much more if we had an open door to both sides of the political aisle and, in fact, we have."

One of the ways WIPP built such a large constituency was by partnering with a variety of women's organizations from around the county. "We felt it was important to bring all the significant women's business associations together for unity," Terry explains. "Some of the associations would hardly speak to each other, much less sit at the same table. That was in 2001; today that is not the case!

"We are all working together through this partnership to ensure that we have a voice in our nation's capital. We also believe these women's associations trust WIPP and know we have integrity and that we work hard every day to continue to earn that trust and integrity. We also are team players. We don't ask any of the association leaders to do anything we wouldn't do. We also play fair and we deliver!"

Barbara adds, "Once we positioned our need to speak as a unified voice in order to make an impact, it was an easy sell. Everyone wanted and needed to participate.

"Women are the best at developing and expanding alliances and strategic partnerships. We all have a common goal: to grow our businesses and make money. We don't need to reinvent the wheel; we need to build on our unique, individual strengths by being inclusive, strategic and smart. If we work together, we all benefit and we will all grow."

For more information on WIPP's efforts to lobby on behalf of women in business, visit www.wipp.org.

I am also a member of the Board of Directors of the Women Presidents' Organization (WPO), and its 501(c)(3) nonprofit arm, the Women Presidents' Educational Organization, is a WBENC organizational partner providing certification in New York, Northern New Jersey and Southwestern Connecticut as well as the tri-state area around Washington, DC. WPO members, women business owners whose revenues must exceed $2 million, are excellent candidates for the certification and other programs provided by WBENC. WBENC and the WPO recently joined forces to launch another program for fast growth woman-owned firms, Zenith, that will work to maximize the effectiveness and competitiveness of WBE firms with revenues in excess of $50 million. (More information on the Zenith Group and criteria for membership can be found in Appendix B.) The programs and benefits of Zenith will depend on the unique capabilities and reach of WBENC and the WPO. The partnership works because we each bring a specific skill set to the table that in turn benefits both the WBE participants and the corporate sponsors of the Zenith Group.

Another organization with which WBENC frequently collaborates is the Center for Women's Business Research, whose statistics on women-owned businesses help us to make the business case for corporations to do business with women. The Center conducts WBENC's Benchmarking Study that tracks the standards in supplier diversity programs and conducted our landmark Access to Markets study, the results of which were released in 2003. Currently, we are working with the Center on a study of women in non-traditional industries.

On a national level, I meet frequently with the Executive Director of the National Association of Women Business Owners (NAWBO), and WBENC's women's business organizational partners (see Appendix C for a complete listing with contact information) work with NAWBO's state and local chapters throughout the country. A similar relationship exists between WBENC and the U.S. Hispanic Chamber of Commerce, and WBENC's local affiliates and the U.S. Hispanic Chamber's local and state chambers around the country.

All of these partnerships provide value to WBENC by providing programs, products and services that are of value to our members. We can expose WBEs to peer advisory groups by referring them to the WPO and, in so doing, make them better suppliers for our corporate members. We can pool our power with that of others by providing a strong voice in Washington's political corridors through WIPP. We can accelerate the certification and contracts for Hispanic women by partnering with the U.S. Hispanic Chamber of Commerce. Each relationship is "win-win-win."

These partnerships also offer a win for the corporations that support each of our organizations. We try very hard to collaborate, but not overlap services and programs. We schedule our major events so as to maximize opportunities rather than create conflict. We know it is important to our corporate partners that we use their financial support wisely and do not duplicate programs across organizations. Our collaboration brings more support to the table for everyone

As you can see from the WBENC example, partnerships exist on many levels and require creative thinking, strategic planning, adaptive skills and an enormous amount of communication and networking. Look carefully at your own circle and I am certain that you will find advisors, suppliers, industry peers and organizations that you rely on for management advice, referrals to clients and suppliers, information on industry trends, leads for attracting employees and services that make your company more efficient. This book will provide advice on how you can use that circle to help you grow your business and accelerate your company's success in the corporate supply chain.

The Building Blocks of Partnership

Now that you have some insight into my experience with partnership as President of WBENC, let us widen the lens and discuss the key elements to keep in mind regarding any partnership relationship. I call them the Building Blocks of Partnership and they will recur throughout the book in a variety of ways. These building blocks represent the five essential elements that must be in place for a partnership to survive and thrive:

1. Timing

Is there a need in the marketplace for the products or services your partnership is planning to offer? Is the time right, professionally and personally, for you and your partner(s) to join forces? Are your prospective clients ready? Have you given adequate thought and planning to the required changes in the infrastructure of your company?

2. Financial Resources

Is this a partnership, a merger, and acquisition or an alliance? What are the specific costs of entering into each? Have you lined up the appropriate financing to complete the deal? Have you consulted with your accountant and/or a trusted financial advisor?

3. Human Capital

What staff do you have to hire? To fire? Have you analyzed the role of new positions or changes in geographic locations? How will economies of scale and elimination of duplicative business functions change your current and future staffing needs? Will retraining key employees be part of the equation? Are current executives prepared and qualified for the management challenges of a larger entity?

4. Support Networks

What advice is available from your trade association? Chamber of Commerce? WBENC and its partners? Your professional mentors and business advisors? Do you need to certify the new entity and, if so, have you planned for how long that will take? Do you have support from friends and family to keep you grounded?

WORDS OF WISDOM

"It is important to acknowledge partnering with your family, your spouse. It is easy for the business to take every hour of 24 hours; for your own personal renewal, you need relationships.
- Marilyn Carlson Nelson, CEO, Carlson Companies

5. Strategic Vision

Do you have a strategic plan to carry out the alliance and maximize its impact on revenues? Have you thought through how this partnership or alliance will affect your goals, plans and product development? What is your exit strategy for the partnership?

JUST-IN-TIME LEARNING: Corporations Need You, Too!

Keep in mind that GMEs are not the only ones who benefit from partnerships and alliances. Corporations benefit too. When you form alliances to meet their needs, they benefit from your increased competitiveness. They also need to meet their diversity requirements, and the more you can help them meet this need in a cost-effective, value-added way, the more business you will win.

Here are some tips from Carol Danoff, Vice President, Non-Product Procurement and Strategic Sourcing, at Pitney Bowes. Carol serves as Chair of WBENC's Strategic Sourcing Committee, which we established in response to the increasing compression of the corporate supply chain.

- **Make sure there is a fit.** "Every corporation is motivated to do businesses with a small business. We want nothing more than to do business with a qualified small business. We get measured all the time so we are always looking for new suppliers. But making that easy for us falls into the hands of the small business. With WBENC or NMSDC certification, you have added access, but is still important that you do your homework. Don't try to do business with a company where there isn't a good match, or where the company does not buy what you sell. With the Internet, so much information is online that there is no excuse for not being prepared. Good preparation will help you understand whether a potential corporate customer is focused on supplier reduction or rationalization. You need to find out if they are looking at expanding their supply base, perhaps in a certain category. It is frustrating to us on the corporate side when there is no real match. Before you make the effort to form an alliance whose purpose is to address our specific needs, call us and ask the right questions. We need to know at the outset that you are aware of our needs and goals and there is a good fit."

- **Focus on creating *solutions* for the corporation.** According to Carol, "People often get confused and think you need to partner with someone in the same space and combine your companies and get bigger. But I think alliances that work put a solution together. It is most important to combine your skills with someone with complementary skills and product offerings."
- **It is not all about price.** "Price does matter," says Carol, "but if you are an efficient small business, you should be able to compete. Many times I see a smaller business being more nimble and competitive than many larger companies. For example, you should look at how you can use technology effectively to be more price-competitive and to leverage some of the resources available to small businesses."

As I mentioned in the Introduction, I find it virtually impossible to talk about mutual support and respect in partnerships without broaching the subject of personal partnerships—and, in particular, marriage. Many of the men and women interviewed for this book also raised this interesting and appropriate comparison. While researching and writing the book, it struck me that much of the advice for successful business partnerships mirrors popular culture advice for successful marriages. Many of the clichés about dating and marriage simply and effectively convey the advice we will present for the development of business relationships. We hope the comparisons will make you laugh, but also help you to understand the dynamics of business partnerships.

To begin the comparisons, I was quite struck by the following list of "components important to successful long-term marriages," based on research conducted by John Gottman, Ph.D., professor of psychology at the University of Washington, and explained in his book, *The Seven Principles for Making a Marriage Work* (with co-author Nan Silver, Crown Publishers, 1999). I find that, excluding number 10 (except in husband-wife businesses, of course), these are excellent partnership tenets to keep in mind when you think about creating and maintaining positive business relationships:

Keys to a Successful Marriage/Relationship
By John Gottman

1. They are gentle with each other.
2. They spend time in and enjoy conversation with each other.
3. They allow for influence by their partner.
4. They do keep score by remembering the good things their partner does for them.
5. Each partner knows himself or herself reasonably well.
6. Each partner honors the other's dreams.
7. There is a positive sense of humor in the relationship.
8. There are shared goals and a sense of teamwork in the relationship.
9. There are good conflict resolution skills in the relationship. (Sometimes this means doing something, and sometimes it means letting things take care of themselves.)
10. There is a sense of continued romance in the relationship.
11. Contempt, for the partner, in all its forms, will more than anything else bring the relationship down. It needs to be avoided or worked through.

Let us review these, one by one, applying each concept to professional partnerships.

1. They are gentle with each other.

It is as important to maintain common courtesies in a business relationship as it is in your personal life. A respectful relationship with your business partners should be a given. None of us is perfect, at least not all of the time. It is important that partners feel free to discuss any issue that may arise without worrying about being criticized or ridiculed.

2. They spend time in and enjoy conversation with each other.

Building on number one, partners need to communicate on a regular basis and they need to get along. Even if partners never socialize beyond the walls of the office, a cordial relationship that encourages dialogue is a key element of a successful business relationship. Important business information frequently is learned through informal discussion. We often get so busy doing what we do and applying what we know that we do not always understand that others, even our partners in life or business, are unaware of the scope of our knowledge or experience. The same, of course, is true concerning our knowledge of our partner's experiences and knowledge.

3. They allow for influence by their partner

If this is a partnership, and not an acquisition, the intent is to bring the skills and resources of each of the partners to the table. If one side dominates, then the partnership is not maximizing its effectiveness. The communication emphasized above can lead to a better understanding of how to maximize the influence of each partner.

4. They do keep score by remembering the good things their partner does for them.

It is important that partners understand the contributions each brings to the table. When you formed your alliance, you did so for a reason, based on your prior experience with your partner. For the partnership to flourish, you need to constantly add to the list and have a body of reasons why the partnership continues to work and why you would "marry" again today.

5. Each partner knows himself or herself reasonably well.

Just as you need to know yourself before entering a marriage—what your vision of the future might be (where you want to live, how you want to live from a material perspective) and what your shared values are—so must you understand yourself as an entrepreneur and business leader. Do you want your company to provide you with riches? A prominent position in the community? An interesting and challenging career that relies more on intellectual stimulation than financial reward? Or do you want to build a company quickly, sell it and then start another business?

6. Each partner honors the other's dreams.

Once you have decided that there are sufficient reasons to get together, you need to keep reminding yourself not just of the reasons that you entered into this alliance, but of the reasons your partner has as well. You need not be Siamese twins joined at the hip—differences often add strength to your partnership—but you need to validate the reasons your partner joined forces with you and your dreams.

7. There is a positive sense of humor in the relationship.

There will be bad days; there will be disappointments. In any relationship there are ruts in the road to success. They are easier to bear and will be put behind you faster if you maintain a global vision and a sense of humor.

8. There are shared goals and a sense of teamwork in the relationship.

It goes without saying that, before formalizing any relationship, you have fully discussed your goals. Are you teaming to provide scope and scale? What commitments has each member of the team made to reach that goal? Are you both willing to let go of being the boss all the time?

9. There are good conflict resolution skills in the relationship. (Sometimes this means doing something, and sometimes it means letting things take care of themselves.)

This is a very important area that is often neglected in the glow of launching your partnership. Any mature individual knows that you and your partner will not agree on everything. As mentioned above, your differences add strength to the relationship. Sometimes, however, those differences can ignite conflict. Just as marriage counselors recommend that a husband and wife never go to bed angry with one another, business partners need to establish rules and procedures for resolving differences.

10. There is a sense of continued romance in the relationship.

Celebrate victories and anniversaries. Include your employees and your clients in your "romance." My former boss, President Ronald Reagan, used to advise that there was no limit to what you could accomplish if you were willing to share the credit. On the advice of marketing guru, WBE Nancy Michaels, last year WBENC sent Valentines to our corporate members, partner organizations and their key staff people, as well as our vendors and consultants. The theme of the missive was that we "loved" them all and valued their role in our success. Rather than getting lost in a pile of holiday cards in December, our Valentines were read and appreciated as a special treat in February.

11. Contempt, for the partner, in all its forms, will more than anything else bring the relationship down. It needs to be avoided or worked through.

Carol Danoff, quoted above, says that speaking ill of your partner is like complaining about your husband's faults to your mother—then she is always skeptical of him in the future! Nothing can destroy the purpose of your alliance faster than speaking ill of your current or potential partners with a current or potential client.

Building Block in Depth: Timing

Because the above principles apply to an existing relationship, in this book I will also add essential guidance for deciding to enter into a partnership in the first place—a topic I will explore in great detail in Chapter Three. For starters, I would like to delve into the first building block of partnership: timing. How often have you heard the phrase "The timing was right," or its opposite, "The timing was just not right"? I know my mother would say to me, when a treasured relationship faltered, that the timing was just not right in an attempt to remove blame from either side of the relationship equation. It is of vital importance that you understand the importance of the timing for entering into a partnership. One of your first questions in deciding a partnership path for you and your business will be, "Is it time for me to enter into a partnership or strategic alliance?" Timing may also, as you will see, be an important factor in ending a relationship. To illustrate this point, I will share one of my own stories about timing.

When I started a consulting company in the mid-1990s, I did what many entrepreneurs do: I took my former employer as a client. Well, sort of. I had run a regional women's business development center for five years in Washington, DC. It was one of the first four "demonstration sites" funded by the Office of Women's Business Ownership at the U.S. Small Business

Administration (SBA). The parent organization of the DC center was the American Woman's Economic Development Corporation (AWED), headquartered in New York City. In the beginning, the Center dealt mostly with women who had either just started their business, mostly out of their homes part-time while still holding down a full-time job elsewhere, or were in the first stage of trying to grow their companies.

It was enormously gratifying to me to see many of these companies succeed over the years. They added employees, moved to professional space and applied for working-capital lines of credit and equipment purchase and real estate loans. I also observed that many of the businesses eventually sought to do business in corporate America and with the Federal government. Yet it seemed they were hitting the same sort of "glass ceiling" that women in corporate America faced. Even a decade ago the disparity between the number of woman-owned firms and the percentage of corporate and government contracts they received was striking. My research determined that women could benefit from supplier development programs like those dedicated to helping minority owned businesses. I felt that one of the keys to making this happen was to create a nationally respected and broadly accepted certification for women's business enterprises, similar to the one provided by the National Minority Supplier Development Council, the main body certifying minority business owners. In my mind, the time was right.

I proposed to AWED that our DC regional center develop a pilot project for certification of women's business enterprises. They were not interested in pursuing this program that I believed was a critical component of growth for woman-owned firms. So, I gave notice to my local Board of Advisors and struck out on my own. We clearly were not on the same page! I felt that we no longer shared a vision for the future; it was necessary to part ways.

Within a year, the DC office of AWED was no more. The local board, however, was still committed to providing training and counseling for local women business owners and those contemplating business ownership. They retained me, newly established in my consulting practice, to write the funding proposal to the SBA to reactivate the center under new leadership. I did, and the SBA funded the *new* center.

The board then approached me to develop a major strategic plan for the new center. "Piece of Cake!" I thought. Based on my five years of experience running AWED, I developed a proposal that addressed funding, staffing, programs and policies. I cleared my work calendar to be free to dig right in on this project, and then sat back and waited for the call.

A long month later I heard back from the board. They said they liked the plan in general, but asked if I could tweak it to include a few additional items. I was not one hundred percent certain they needed the additional information at that time, but they were my prospective partners in this project, so I rewrote the proposal and scope of work to accommodate the client's needs.

I submitted my rewritten proposal and once again another month passed before I received feedback. I was still reluctant to book my time elsewhere because this was a large contract, and one near and dear to my heart. I totally believed that the timing was perfect for both me and my partner—the client. I expected a signing date for the contract and an advance on the contract amount, which was $30,000; at that time, a significant contract for my business. I was disappointed when once again they asked me to make several revisions, this time more extensive than the previous request. This happened two more times. I should have known right then that the timing was off and, more important, they did not respect my time. It did not appear as though we were communicating effectively, nor did we fully understand one another's goals. I had not written the proposal in a vacuum; I had interviewed several members of the board and was responding to their stated needs; at least what I thought I heard them state their needs to be. Unfortunately, like a commitment-phobic suitor, they kept changing their minds about what they wanted.

After the fourth revision the proposal was no longer something I recognized or even endorsed. I wondered if this "marriage made in heaven" would ever make it to the altar.

At this point I can honestly say I was getting very nervous. If I were to carry out the terms of the revised contract as a sole proprietor, I would have to devote a significant amount of time to this project. I had not planned well for the negotiation time required to iron out the details. I had not defined my timing and had not planned properly for all of the factors that were driving this relationship. More important, with each revision that rolled out of the printer, the less my desire was to actually work on a project that no longer resembled my original proposal. Did we really have the same goals and shared values?

For example, I had recommended a fundraising strategy that would be carried out by various members of the board, based on their personal and professional contacts. The board, however, wanted me to do the fundraising on my own, just as I had done when I was a paid employee of the former AWED organization. Furthermore, they wanted to restrict my ability to raise funds for any other organization. They demanded that if I approached a corporation or foundation on their behalf, I could not go back to the same organization for any other client.

Finally, I asked the board member with whom I was dealing if I could meet with the entire board. I told them that I was going to turn down the contract. I briefed them on my reasons: 1) I did not think the revised proposal would create a successful product and they would not be satisfied with the result. 2) I was not happy with the conditions they were setting that limited my work for other clients. 3) I felt that, as a new business, I could not afford to have a *failure* or unhappy clients, especially unhappy clients who were my friends. Even though I was $45,000 into the $50,000 line of credit I had taken out to launch my business, I felt terrific walking out of that meeting after turning down that $30,000 contract.

On the surface, my decision does not make much sense. These women were all professional friends of mine. I had worked with them on shared goals and programs at AWED. Together, we had developed a successful grant application to SBA. I respected them and liked them. We had shared values, an important factor in any relationship, whether it is client and supplier or formal partner. We had worked successfully together in the past. This sounds like a winning scenario, but it was not. Why? Timing.

The timing in this situation was clearly off, as was our communication. Have you ever tried to date an old boyfriend or girlfriend and come away wondering what you ever saw in him or her in the first place? While we had worked together in the past, we could not move to the new reality as a team. The romance was over. I did not understand that the board members wanted to create a new *brand* that showcased their leadership, not just a rebirth of the old organization. They did not understand that they could not go to an independent consultant and make demands inappropriate to a supplier/client relationship. They were still dealing with me as though I were their employee. I was still dealing with them as though I was the Executive Director and they were my board. Furthermore, they did not understand the role of a consultant and the *time is money* theory.

As you can see from my story, partnerships are never a guaranteed success, even when prospective partners have worked together in the past. Because the timing was off, the partnership could not move ahead.

Remember that even if it is not the right time for you to enter into a partnership, it is always the right time to have partnering on your mind. Life changes very quickly, especially in the world of business, so the more prepared you are for opportunities, the more likely you are to find them.

Chapter Two:

Partnership and You

WORDS OF WISDOM

"Nobody can do 100 percent of anything! But, when partnerships are forged, suddenly there is no limit to the accomplishments that might be achieved."

- Kathy Greco, Director of Supplier Diversity, Manpower Professional

No man or woman is an island, and no business can exist in isolation either. Partnerships, alliances and collaborations are essential to the success of any organization, from sole proprietors to multi-national corporations to governments and nonprofit organizations. "Bringing on a paid board at the beginning was the single best decision I made," says WBE Pat Henriquez of Management Alternatives, whose Profitable Partnership profile appeared in Chapter One. "I took a look at the gaps in my own background and through my contacts looked for people who could bring knowledge of that area to the table. I always had a lawyer, marketing guru and a general business adviser. Because I paid them, I could call them in between meetings for advice. When we expanded into the federal government sector, I found someone with federal contracting experience at a high level and another who understood the complexities of federal pricing."

As I have stated, I believe in and will address a wide array of definitions for the term "partner," including customers, suppliers, funders, employees, advisors, certification organizations and membership associations. However, *Partnering for Profit* is primarily designed to expose you to the varying forms of partnerships for the purpose of jointly serving the customer and increasing your profitability.

In the world of the supplier diversity marketplace, in which most readers of this book do business, you will most often hear this situation referred to as "strategic alliances." *Strategic* is a key word, and as I have emphasized from the outset, the purpose of looking beyond your current capabilities is to position you and your business as a more attractive partner in tomorrow's supply chain. Remember that "Strategic Vision" is one of the essential building blocks of partnership.

Honoring the importance of communication among partners (and of course you and I are partners, dear reader!), before we go any farther I would like to pause here to define some terms that will appear frequently throughout this book.

Growth Market Enterprise

In *Breaking Through,* I proposed renaming all "minority" supplier business classifications as **Growth Market Enterprises (GMEs)**. As I wrote in my earlier book, this term captures the present and future of the new face of business in America. The new name also provides a realistic and positive descriptive that connotes business capability, progress and deliverability. These businesses are not "disadvantaged" or "minor," but represent the new demographic landscape of both America's business community and the country's consumer base. They reflect the diversity and promise of our country.

Furthermore, GME incorporates women, minority and other identifications, combining several very powerful communities and building strength in our combined numbers. While you will not see the term GME used in corporate or government supplier diversity literature (not yet, anyway), I will use the phrase throughout *Partnering for Profit* as the most inclusive way to define the businesses that can benefit from corporate supplier diversity initiatives and the strategies I will recommend.

Strategic Alliance

While "partnership" is a very specific legal term with a plethora of requirements, "strategic alliance" has a more inclusive and flexible definition. You may hear this phrase used by large corporations referring to their highest-level vendor relationships (e.g., Dell may refer to a strategic alliance with Intel, because Dell computers carry Intel processors), but in this book I will use the term's more inclusive definition. Consider this explanation from management consulting firm Bain & Company:*

> ***Strategic Alliances** are agreements between firms in which each commits resources to achieve a common set of objectives. Companies may form Strategic Alliances with a wide variety of players: customers, suppliers, competitors, universities or divisions of government. Through Strategic Alliances, companies can improve competitive positioning, gain entry to new markets, supplement critical skills, and share the risk or cost of major development projects. Strategic Alliances are formed to:*

- *Reduce costs through economies of scale or increased knowledge;*
- *Increase access to new technology;*
- *Inhibit competitors;*
- *Enter new markets;*
- *Reduce cycle time;*
- *Improve research and development efforts;*
- *Improve quality.*

---

* "Strategic Alliances," in "Management Tools 2003: An Executive's Guide," Bain & Company, 2003.

I also like this definition provided by Bill Robinson of RelentlessMarketing.com, writing for Forbes.com:

[Strategic alliances are] very close business relationships between two companies for their mutual benefit. What any organization that participates in a strategic alliance wants is access to another company's strengths, whether they be in distribution, technology, sales, manufacturing or marketing, in exchange for providing some support, resources or access to a missing ingredient for that partner.

Teaming

Teaming was a popular term in the early 1990s, used frequently to describe opportunities to bid on government contracts and to differentiate the relationship from that of tiered "subcontractor" to one of equals working together. According to Federal Access (*www.fedaccess.com*), "Teaming agreements... involve two or more parties agreeing to jointly pursue a contract or group of contracts." Management Alternatives, profiled in Chapter One, used teaming arrangements for their entry into the public sector: "When we expanded to the federal sector, we got heavily involved in teaming arrangements," says founder Pat Henriquez. "At times we were on several teams going after the same contract. We were too small to do exclusives. It worked for us because we had a reputation for confidentiality. We would not disclose the terms of one bid to another team."

JUST-IN-TIME LEARNING: Government Advice on Teaming and Joint Ventures

While Partnering for Profit offers a wide range of definitions of partnership, the federal government is much more specific. Familiarize yourself with this more detailed information to gain a deeper understanding of how teaming arrangements and joint ventures might benefit your business.

First are some basic guidelines for using "Contractor Team

Arrangements" from the U.S. General Services Administration (GSA):

Federal Supply Schedule Contractors may use "Contractor Team Arrangements" (see FAR 9.6) to provide solutions when responding to ordering activity requirements. These Team Arrangements can be included under a Blanket Purchase Agreement (BPA). BPAs are permitted under all Federal Supply Schedule contracts. Orders under a Team Arrangement are subject to terms and conditions or the Federal Supply Schedule Contract. Participation in a Team Arrangement is limited to Federal Supply Schedule Contractors.

Here is a general outline on how teaming works:

The customer identifies their requirements.

Federal Supply Schedule Contractors may individually meet the customers' needs, or Federal Supply Schedule Contractors may individually submit a "Team Solution" to meet the customer's requirement.

Customers make a best value selection.

Additional advice, definitions and differentiation of terms is provided below from the SBA's Office of Government Contracting's Contract Assistance for Women Business Owners (CAWBO) unit:

Measures to Facilitate Teaming Arrangements

A significant way to increase contract opportunities for Women-Owned Small Businesses (WOSBs) is through teaming arrangements and subcontracting relationships. Teaming arrangements are desirable from a federal and industry standpoint because they enable the companies involved to complement each other's unique capabilities and offer the government the best combination of performance, cost, and delivery for the product being acquired. WOSB teaming agreements may include large businesses or other small businesses. There may be size issues involved when small businesses enter teaming agreements. It is recommended that a small business contemplating a teaming agreement consult with an attorney that specializes in that area before entering into any such arrangement.

What is a Teaming Arrangement?

The Federal Acquisition Regulation (FAR) Subpart 9.6, Contractor Team Arrangements, describes contractor team arrangements as follows: "Two or more companies form a partnership or joint venture to act as a potential prime contractor"; or "A potential prime contractor agrees with one or more other companies to have them act as its subcontractors under a specified Government contract or acquisition program."

What is a Major Difference Between a Partnership and a Joint Venture?

A partnership is a voluntary association of two or more individuals to carry on a business for profit, usually on a permanent basis. A limited partnership provides for limited liability of one or more of the partners. A joint venture consists of two or more companies combining their resources to form a new company, as a separate entity from the existing companies, for the purpose of performing a contract. Once the contract is completed, the joint venture is dissolved along with the new company that was formed to perform the contract.

What Does The Teaming Process Involve?

To establish teaming arrangements, small businesses or large and small businesses combine their resources to bid on major procurements. The companies may combine their financial capabilities, managerial and technical skills, personnel, business facilities and/or equipment to become a successful bidder on a contract. A review of the proposed documents by an attorney knowledgeable about teaming agreements is highly recommended.

Teaming with another company involves finding the right partner. In addition to combining your products and services with your partner's products and services, it is recommended that you research your potential partner's financial condition. Check the credit history of the company, working capital, past performance and current teaming relationships. You must also know your partner's economic viability and identify your firm's strengths, weaknesses, and future goals.

Participants in teaming and subcontracting agreements should be knowledgeable about the standard terms and conditions of the agreement. Questions regarding claims, the small business size status of the participants, regulations, federal policy, state laws, legislation, reimbursement, payment, licenses, responsibility and obligation should be addressed before entering into the teaming agreement. As a result, consulting with an attorney and reviewing relevant legal documents and possible areas of concern or dispute can be helpful before entering into teaming and subcontracting arrangements. This may help to identify the problems and solutions that teaming and subcontracting arrangements present.

What Benefits Can I Expect From Teaming Arrangements?

For WOSBs, teaming with a prime contractor has many benefits, including the opportunity to: (1) increase annual profits; (2) work on large government procurements; (3) increase working capital; (4) gain experience with a diverse workforce; (5) expand and/or diversify products; (6) network to develop strong business relationships; (7) realize advancements in management and technical skills; and (8) increase contract awards.

The Office of Small and Disadvantaged Business Utilization (OSDBU) in each federal agency has information about how to market your company to find teaming arrangements. You may connect to each of the OSDBU offices through several web sites, including the WomenBiz.gov site located at www.womenbiz.gov , the Department of the Treasury at www.ustreas.gov/sba, and the Department of Commerce at www.osec.doc.gov/osdbu.

Most of the OSDBU offices' web sites list contact names and telephone numbers. You can contact one of the small business specialists in the OSDBU office to discuss your company's teaming needs. The small business specialist will be able to assist you with information about what types of procurements are available for your products or services now and in the future.

See Appendix C for contact information for the Offices of Small and Disadvantaged Business Utilization in the Federal Government.

Why is Partnership So Important?

When my collaborator, Lindsey Pollak, and I began conducting interviews for this book, we were struck, although not at all surprised, at the response to the topic of strategic alliances. With corporate supply chains shrinking in all industries and product and service categories, certified business owners and supplier diversity executives alike are aware that GMEs have no choice but to partner with other companies to remain viable candidates for corporate contracts; and, regardless of supply chain issues, partnership is one of the most common and successful strategies for business growth in general. As Keith Hines, former Manager of Corporate Purchasing at Altria and now director of purchasing at Cushman Wakefield, states quite simply about alliances at every level, "If you are savvy enough to realize the benefits, it is how most people grow."

If you are a smaller business owner who has never been able to win a corporate contract, partnering may provide the winning strategy. As I wrote in my first book, *Breaking Through*, corporations are always on the lookout for seamless service, and one way for smaller GMEs to break into the supply chain is to make it your business to package the skills, products or logistics of several other companies—sometimes referred to as being a "business solution partner." By integrating an entire solution and offering several services in one package, you make life easier for a corporate buyer who does not want 20 relationships requiring 20 invoices and 20 phone calls a day.

JUST-IN-TIME LEARNING: An Emerging Trend

The Center for Women's Business Research, which defines itself as the "premier source of knowledge about women business owners and their enterprises worldwide," offers this assessment of the importance of strategic alliances and other partnerships to women entrepreneurs wanting to grow their businesses:

"The formation of strategic alliances is also a trend emerging in response to 'bundling.' Bundling is the practice of combining several individual projects or potential contracts into a single large contract in order to reduce costs and improve administration efficiency. Strategic alliances are partnerships between two or more firms with complementary products or services. The alliance allows the partners to bid on larger, bundled contracts. Partners might also be able to bid on contracts more competitively as an alliance than if they each did so on their own.

"An example of a strategic alliance might include a design firm, a writer and a printer combining skills and resources to bid on a marketing piece. Corporate purchasing representatives encourage women business owners to create strategic alliances in order to boost their competitive advantage."

For more information and business tips, visit www.womensbusinessresearch.org.

You, Inc.

Before we continue in our discussion of partnerships, we need to talk about what is likely one of your favorite topics: you. Before you can think about what kind of partner or partners you will need to grow your business, you must honestly assess the current state of your company and your role as its leader. Do not forget the building blocks we discussed in Chapter One. Is the timing right for you and your business? Have you evaluated your resources lately, both from the financial perspective as well as human resources? Are you a "catch," or do you need to take remedial action before exploring an alliance? The more you know about your business needs, your personal style and your future goals, the better partnership plan you can pursue. Remember that partnership involves two levels of success: entering into the right partnerships and then managing those partnerships once they exist. Both of these levels have one common denominator: you.

I thought it would be fun to think about this self-assessment chapter as you might approach an online dating profile. The more accurately and candidly you can describe yourself and your needs, the more likely you are to attract a truly perfect match. (And I happen to know that more than a few WBENC-certified women of all ages have found dates and mates through matchmaking web sites!) Online dating profiles include a series of questions—some essay, some multiple choice—that provide the basis for matching people with each other. This chapter follows the same structure, asking you a series of crucial questions to guide you to create a profile that you can use later in this book when we begin to discuss various partnership options.

You will note that some of the questions are purely business-related and some assess your personality traits and individual style. Both professional and personal factors contribute to the success or failure of a partnership, so pay them equal attention. It is quite similar to the process of hiring an employee for your business. Recently, I was recruiting a new executive assistant and called on Lynne Marie Finn of Superior Staffing Services, Inc. to provide guidance and a professional perspective. As background, for three years in the 1980s I was an Associate Director of Presidential Personnel at The White House. I made quite a reputation for myself in getting to the nitty-gritty of what made a good match among background, history and current opportunity. I knew how to pick the perfect executive to serve a specific role in government and did equally well identifying support staff and matching them effectively with those executives.

As I have learned, however, I am not alone in the flat-out and undeniable inability to identify and interview an Executive Assistant for myself. This is a crucial role in the WBENC office and, I must admit, when I am not happy it is not a good thing! My Executive Assistant is responsible for keeping me happy: making certain that calls are answered effectively, schedules set, research conducted on trips and meetings and correspondence kept up to date. Lynne came to our office, interviewed me and my direct reports to get a clearer picture of not only the basic items in the job description, but also what my personal characteristics were as a boss and the general tone and pace of the office Lynne was a terrific partner in this process. Having her handle the search and make the recommendation of a final candidate could not have gone more smoothly. It was as though she knew me better than I know myself.

If you do not believe that personal issues are really that important to business relationships, just think about the interpersonal issues of the infighting between former friends Michael Eisner and Michael Ovitz that cost the Disney Corporation millions of dollars. Even partnerships at the highest levels of Corporate America and international politics are, at the end of the day, relationships among people.

Your very first assignment is to complete the following self-assessment. Then, in the next chapter, we will begin to think about criteria for your perfect match. As we progress through later chapters, I will walk you through the steps of finding companies that fit your match criteria, negotiating an alliance or partnership relationship, working together effectively and growing or ending the partnership if need be. Rest assured that all of this information is presented with special attention paid to the unique perspective of women and minority business owners.

Partnering for Profit Self-Assessment Part I: Business Basics

WORDS OF WISDOM

"He who knows others is learned. He who knows himself is wise." - Lao Tzu

Now, let us create your profile. Keep in mind that the goal of these questions is for you to develop a clear sense of where you and your company are at this point. The better you know yourself (and the more honest you are in your assessment), the better you will be able to identify the right partner or partners and communicate to them what they will want to know about your company.

What are the core products or services of your business today?

What is your unique selling proposition? What do you do better than anyone else?

What new customers are you seeking?

It is a commonly held rule that 80 percent of a company's business often comes from 20 percent of its customers. Will your company grow by expanding your customer base, by winning new business from existing customers, or both? Answering this fundamental question will help later decisions about whether a horizontal or vertical partnership is most appropriate for you.

Are there any additional products or services that your customers have requested that you are not yet providing?

If nothing comes to mind, consider surveying your current customers (especially those with whom you have a close working relationship) to ask what else they might be interested in purchasing from you. You will never know until you ask, and you may find that their requests are quite reasonable. General market research techniques will also provide a clear picture of what the company buys and from whom. You can come up with your own analysis of what broader array of products or services might fit well with your own product or service mix. From a strategic sourcing perspective, it is also important to analyze both the competition and your most important customers' purchasing profile. It may not be enough to ask, "What else do you want to buy from me?" The proper question might be, "At what point will I lose the contract if I don't increase scale or scope?"

Have you ever lost out on a contract with a corporation or other customer? If so, what reason(s) did they give for the rejection?

Do not assume that you lost a contract with a big corporation because you are not big enough. A variety of factors may have played a role, including geographic capability, technological misalignment and cultural fit. If you do not know why you lost certain bids, by all means contact the supplier diversity professional with whom you interacted to find out the reasons why. This can offer crucial information about the partnerships you might need to pursue in order to win a similar contract in the future. Remember that every rejection contains an opportunity—and probably an opportunity for partnership.

What is your geographic reach?

Is your reach local, regional, national or global? Are you the biggest player in your industry in your area? Do you need to expand into new geographic locations to win more business?

What do you consider to be the biggest weaknesses in your company right now? What have you done to address these weaknesses up to this point?

The more honest you are about your shortcomings, the more you will be able to seek partners who can fill in the gaps. Remember that every company has weaknesses; no one can do everything.

How would you assess your current technological capabilities?

Multiple choice:

- Cutting-edge for my field. I always seek to implement the most current technology to stay on top of the trends. Business-wise, I consider myself to be an "early adopter."
- I meet the requirements for my industry and upgrade when I need to.
- Adequate. I pretty much have what I need, but no more.
- My technology could use improvement.
- I am dissatisfied with the technology I have for my business.
- Technology? What is technology?

List your current business partners. How happy are you with each relationship and are you interested in a new relationship in any of these areas?

For each category, write down the name of the partner and your current level of happiness with the relationship:

- Strategic alliances
- Vendors
- Investors/Equity financing
- Bank/Provider of debt

- Attorney
- Accountant
- Business advisors
- Certification organization
- Other professional associations
- Key clients/customers
- Employees

List your competitors and write an honest assessment of their business assets, liabilities and cultures. Could you work with any of your competitors? Have you ever worked with any of your competitors?

Think ExxonMobil. ChevronTexaco. JPMorgan Chase. It is very common for former competitors to join forces. Do not rule out the possibility that today's enemy may become tomorrow's ally. This can have important ramifications if you were doing business with one half of the named companies above but not both. If there are two suppliers with the same product or service one will likely be eliminated. Can your company service the geography and increased scale of the merged corporation? A teaming arrangement with your "competition," the supplier to the other half of the merged company, can head off problems and create that "win-win-win" we spoke of earlier.

Partnering for Profit Self-Assessment Part II: Culture Club

The people who work for you are among your most important constituents in the partnering and business growth process—human capital is a partnership building block no matter how small or large your organization may be. Consider your company culture as a key decision-making factor in any alliance decision.

WORDS OF WISDOM: Employees are Partners, Too

"I consider my employees as partners. As they strive for efficiency, accuracy and conscientious performance they are providing excellent service, which in turn increases our customer base and allows for their own financial gain through being employed by a successful company."
- Charline Guidry
Chairman and CEO, Diamond Oil Field Supply,
Belle Chasse, Louisiana

How would you truthfully characterize the culture of your organization?

Choose as many as apply:

- Collaborative
- Creative
- Disorganized
- Environmentally aware
- Family-friendly
- Feminine
- Friendly
- Masculine
- Quiet
- Young
- Competitive
- Disciplined
- Entrepreneurial
- Ethical
- Fast-paced
- Flexible
- High turnover
- Old-fashioned
- Team-oriented
- Old school

What human resources do you bring to the table? Are these negotiable?

Now is the time to begin thinking about the effect of various partnerships on your employees. Some questions to ponder:

- How many people do you currently employ? Is this number too few, too many or just right?
- How "formal" is your organization? For instance, how important are titles to your staff members?

- What hours do your employees generally work? Do you offer flexible hours and/or work-from-home situations?
- What is the average age of your staff?
- Who are the key employees you could not imagine living without?
- Are key employees willing to relocate?

What do you consider to be the most important ethical "rules" of your organization? What values are non-negotiable?

Choose all that apply and feel free to add additional values:

- Avoiding conflict of interest
- Commitment
- Environmentalism
- Fiscal responsibility
- Generosity/Charity
- Honesty
- Loyalty
- Spirituality
- Tolerance (diversity awareness)
- Sense of humor
- Intellectual rigor

Partnering for Profit Self-Assessment Part III: Leadership Lowdown

By running a successful business you have demonstrated that you have leadership skills, but how will those "boss" skills translate when you have to share leadership with another entrepreneur? Here are a few questions to help you better understand your leadership style so that you can be honest when discussing an alliance with a potential partner.

What qualities describe your leadership style?

Choose as many as apply:

- Aggressive
- Communicative
- Creative
- Easygoing
- Judgmental
- Sensitive
- Supportive
- Collaborative
- Competitive
- Critical
- Egocentric
- Micro-managing
- Strategic
- Technology-savvy

What do you consider to be your best qualities as a leader?

Think about compliments you have received from clients, employees and others. Do you chair committees or charity drives in your community? Have you been asked to serve on boards of directors or advisory committees for nonprofit or for profit organizations?

In what areas could you use some improvement as a leader?

Again, refer to specific feedback you have received. If you have ever worked with a coach, think back on the areas in which you focused your attention to improve.

To what extent would you be willing to share, or even cede, leadership duties to a partner?

Be honest! Do you need to be the boss? This is particularly important if you are considering a partnership. If you need to be the leader as does your prospective partner, you may want to consider an acquisition (or sale) instead.

Would you be comfortable working with a partner of a different gender, ethnicity, generation, country or management level?

Again, this question requires a strong degree of honesty and self-reflection. Would you be able to work with someone at a middle management level if you partnered with a larger company? Would you be comfortable sharing confidential information with someone 20 years your junior or senior?

In some cases, adding diversity to your ownership can yield extraordinary benefits. For instance, Roz Alford of ASAP Staffing specifically sought out a younger partner in order to secure the longevity of her company. "As part of my ongoing professional development," Roz explains, "I had taken a course on leadership. The instructor had said that if you are a CEO and do not have young people around you, your ideas will become stale. They even suggested specifically that you should have someone around 30 years of age in a key staff position." As you will see in the Profitable Partnership on ASAP Staffing in Chapter Three, Roz found Nancy Williams, and they have been successful partners ever since.

Next Steps

While it can be difficult to take an honest inventory of our businesses, and ourselves, this is an essential step in the partnership process. Congratulations on finishing the hard part! Now that you have a clearer idea of what you bring to the table as a potential partner, the next chapter will address the diverse types of partnerships you might want to consider. Just as I reassure my single friends, you are quite a catch yourself and I promise you there are many fish in the sea—and many different ways to swim together.

Chapter Three

Partners á la Carte: What Kinds of Partnerships Exist?

What is your type? Before I met my husband, I had a long list of what I thought I wanted in a partner. Bearing in mind that I was far from being a child bride, and had already experienced one unsuccessful marriage, I had a pretty good idea of the items on my list. Most of us, in fact, can answer this question down to the smallest detail when it comes to a potential or existing mate, but people often do not spend adequate time thinking about the must-haves before jumping into a business partnership. They should, because the consequences of a divorce in the business world, from both a financial and an emotional perspective, can be as devastating as the breakup of a family. This chapter is designed to maximize your chances of finding the right *type* of partnership for your specific business needs. The next chapter will then guide you through the process of vetting specific partners to fit the *type* of partnership you determine is best.

Because your needs will surely change over time, I invite you to revisit this chapter in the future as you assess potential partnerships—both personal and professional. Remember also that, although you may not currently be interested in a particular type of partnership, acquisition or alliance, you can still benefit from understanding what various partnership relationships entail; you never know when that supply chain opportunity may arise and you find yourself working with a client, vendor or other business involved in one of these types of partnerships.

One more important note: As you read through these partnership descriptions, always keep in mind three golden questions:

- **"What is in if for my customers or clients?"** Since the goal of any partnership is to become more profitable—generate more revenue or decrease overall costs—and strengthen your supply chain position, be sure that you always consider the needs of your current and future customer or client base. If a particular partnership does not serve the needs of your customers and encourage them to do more business with you, then what is the point?
- **"What is in it for me?"** No matter who your partner(s) may be, you must keep your self-interest in mind. If a relationship will not increase your business, save you time or affect you in another positive way, it is not worth your time and effort. More than any other relationship, it must be a win-win for the partners.
- **"What is in it for my partner?"** For a partnership to be successful, it must benefit both partners. And, it must create added value for your customer. Remember, "win-win-win" is your mantra (see "Words of Wisdom" in this section.)

WORDS OF WISDOM: Win-Win-Win

There is one phrase you will hear over and over when discussing the most successful partnerships in business and in life: win-win. This book will add a third "win" to that phrase. It is no secret that mutually beneficial relationships are the longest lasting and most profitable. No matter what type of alliance you enter into, make sure it is a win-win. Here are some inspiring quotations to keep top-of-mind:

"I have found no greater satisfaction than achieving success through honest dealing and strict adherence to the view

that, for you to gain, those you deal with should gain as well."
- Alan Greenspan, Federal Reserve Chairman

"The most important single central fact about a free market is that no exchange takes place unless both parties benefit."
- Milton Friedman, Nobel Prize-Winning Economist

"Partnership is a relationship that is based on mutual goals, benefits, risks and gains. Both parties must be equally committed to the partnership or it quickly deteriorates."
- Pat Birmingham, Associate Director, Vendor Management, Pfizer Global Sourcing

"To be successful in a business partnership three major components are required: trust, communication and a legal document explaining in detail each partner's duties. These relationships seem to succeed because the 'win-win' issue is addressed prior to the work commencing."
- Judith Ritter, President, Ritter Contracting, Inc., Southampton, Pennsylvania

Timing: A Reason, a Season or a Lifetime?

As you learned in Chapter One, I believe that timing is one of the most important building blocks in any kind of partnership. A friend of mine likes to say that people come into your life for "a reason, a season or a lifetime" and I think that is an excellent starting point when assessing a potential partnership. To extend the relationship analogy: is this a date, a long-term relationship or a marriage? Are you looking for a partner to bid on a specific opportunity that has a defined beginning and end; to expand a specific niche of your existing business, but not the entire span of your business scale and scope; or an integrated and permanent partner for your strategic growth plan? Or, is it something else entirely?

As you know, timing has a lot to do with whom you find. Are you looking for Prince or Princess Charming or just an escort to the ball?

Partnership for a **reason** might include:

- Forming a strategic alliance on a particular contract (partnership with a Growth Market Enterprise [GME] or majority business)
- Increasing your gross revenue floor to bid on larger contracts
- Working with an existing supplier of a target company
- Your client has asked you to enter into a relationship
- You need additional funding to grow your company

Partnership for a **season** might include:

- Forming a relationship with a bank or venture capital firm for funding over a specific period of time
- Partnering with a temporary staffing agency to help staff your business during your busiest time period
- Hiring contract labor to staff a major project (See Profitable Partnership profile in this section)
- Meeting time deadlines for current clients by adding to capacity

PROFITABLE PARTNERSHIP

Stovell Marketing & Public Relations Staffs Up

WBE E. Denise Stovell handles WBENC's public relations and our two annual events, the Salute to Women's Business Enterprises and our annual conference, Women in Business: Sharing the Vision. To handle these large-scale events, Denise's company, Stovell Marketing & Public Relations, partners with other WBEs—some large businesses, some independent contractors—to produce excellent results. Here are her tips, which are especially relevant to small businesses vying for larger accounts:

"Working with staffing agencies is the way to go for small businesses that need to pump up their expert quota on a project-by-project basis. Women-owned businesses excel in this industry as far as I'm concerned. They understand growth spurts and the need to have a flexible team of experts available literally at the snap of a finger, ready and anxious to get the job done right.

"Beware, however, of overpriced expertise...shop around. A treasure chest of resources can be found within the ranks of skilled office managers and executive assistants. I like to offer opportunity to existing staffers to step up and work on new projects. It is an excellent way to maintain employee relations as well as identify fresh talent—right in your own backyard."

Partnership for a **lifetime** might include:

- Partnering with an international company to go global permanently
- Joining forces with a younger firm to ensure the longevity of your business
- Acquiring a company in a new business niche that complements your existing business line (As I write this, I am reading in *The Wall Street Journal* that Johnson & Johnson is acquiring a company that provides scale for an existing line of business and adds a new, up-and-coming product line that, while different from their existing product offerings, is in the same field and would be marketed to the same customers. This is just one reminder that reading business journals can provide you with "just-in-time" access to the strategies being employed by America's largest and most successful companies. If it works for them, it can work for you too.)

- Permanently increasing the geographic scope of your company
- Creating growth economies of scale. The number of mergers and acquisitions announced in the first quarter of 2005 is amazing: Sprint and Nextel, SBC and AT&T, Verizon and MCI, and Procter & Gamble and Gillette are some of the major ones that come to mind. (Examining the published reports on the acquisition of MCI by Verizon and the competitive bids by Qwest, in the headlines as I write this book, show that a simple dollar equation does not always make the best partnership. Stability, scope and credit history were all factors reviewed by MCI management and shareholders.)
- Vertically or horizontally integrating related products or services.

PROFITABLE PARTERNSHIP: Neutral Posture, Inc.

Rebecca Boenigk, CEO and Chairman of the Board of Neutral Posture, Inc., shares her story of the pros and potential cons of vertical teaming alliances:

"About three years ago our largest partner/alliance was with a company called Relax the Back. We were doing over $2 million a year distributing chairs through their franchise network. The corporate office ended up in bankruptcy and we lost over $350,000 because of it. At that point, not only had we lost the money but, we lost the distribution and sales. At about the same time we started teaming with a company called Wrightline. They manufacture lab and office furniture workstations but they do not manufacture seating. Our teaming agreement with them works in the private sector as well as the public sector as we team on our GSA [General Services Administration] contracts as well. We are also looking for similar types of agreements with other companies in different marketing channels."

Is Now the Right Time for You?

As with dating relationships, sometimes opportunities arise when you least expect them. You might be at the supermarket buying a frozen dinner when...BAM! Cupid strikes. Likewise, a business networking event or a meeting with a current or prospective client might suddenly turn into an opportunity for growth and change. No matter what the motive may be for a partnership, how do you determine if the timing is right to even start a discussion? Here are some additional timing tips to think about sooner rather than later in the partnership discussion, particularly if a partnership opportunity arises without your having planned for it:

- Will this partnership serve the current and future needs of your desired customer base? Directly ask your best clients and customers what services, products and efficiencies they need and use this information as the basis for partnership decisions. As I mentioned above, if you are not serving your customers better through an alliance, then what is the point?
- Are you considering this partnership out of financial or emotional desperation? Do not give up the due diligence necessary to any partnership because you feel rushed or pressured. At WBENC, I frequently get calls from a nearly hysterical WBE asking if we can expedite her certification because it is required for a specific business opportunity she is pursuing. WBENC is a partner in this process. The corporation offering the opportunity is our partner as well and expects us to do our job in a professional manner. This means following our processes and not playing favorites. Businesses need to think long term and apply for certification when there is time for a "courtship." We do not do shotgun certification!

JUST-IN-TIME LEARNING: Preparing for Opportunity to Knock

A friend of mine, after a distinguished career that included time with the Department of State and in the Reagan White House, served as Undersecretary of the Air Force in the elder Bush's presidency. At an official event, a woman asked her how she happened to attain that position. Her response: "I worked very, very, very hard for a long, long, long time, and then I got lucky." The message: you have to be ready to move quickly when opportunity comes knocking. Do your homework, dot the "i's," cross the "t's" and when opportunity finds you, you will be ready.

- Are you entering this relationship just because it came along? When someone else approaches you (rather than the other way around), it is easy to feel flattered—or blindsided. Remember, just because an opportunity presents itself does not necessarily mean the partnership is right for you. Due diligence is key to a successful long-term relationship.

WORDS OF WISDOM: Take Your Time

"A lesson I have learned is to not be so eager to create business that I forced a bad fit and got bad press from the association. There is plenty of business to go around, and plenty of good people to partner with. It is worth the effort to make a good choice...It pays to take greater care up front and make sure the match works. Most of us would not get married on the first date because we thought there would be big money in it for us: we would want to make sure the partnership worked first."
- Julia Hubbel
President, The Hubbel Group, Lakewood, Colorado

- Will the partnership take time away from other priorities? Can you or your key staff members devote time to this relationship? If you are too busy with other projects, the partnership may never get past the discussion phase. Remember the "Strategic Vision" in the building blocks? A well thought-out long range plan will help you decide whether you should table current plans to enable you to pursue an important opportunity.
- Speaking of a long-range plan, do you have all of your ducks in a row? All of the building blocks are important here. In addition to an up-to-date certification, when you enter a partnership you will likely be asked to share some important information about your business—financial statements, payroll records, sales figures, for example. If you are not ready to share such information (or have not yet compiled it all for your own uses), you may not be ready for a partner.
- What are the economic conditions in your industry and the local and national marketplace? Do take the time to research such information before becoming involved with a partner, particularly if they are in a region or industry that is foreign to you. This is where your networks come into play and can provide crucial, timely information. Ralph G. Moore of Ralph G. Moore and Associates always emphasizes the importance of the marketplace when he advises GMEs on alliances. "I always tell people to make sure there is a customer at the end—that you are bringing some benefit to the marketplace. For instance, if you were a great buggy whip manufacturer and you partnered with another buggy whip manufacturer, you would still be out of business today!"
- Are you mentally prepared for a partnership? You might think of this an your "ego check." Are you ready

for the possibility that you may not be in charge of certain areas of your business once the partnership begins? Are you comfortable dealing with another company's staff? As we discussed in Chapter Two, do not forget to think about personal issues when assessing every aspect of a potential partnership.

- Is your staff prepared for a partnership at this point in time? Take the pulse of your people: how is morale? Are they overworked? Has there been a lot of change lately in your organization? Remember that you will need staff buy-in to make a partnership work at every level. While many aspects of a deal in progress may have to be held close to the vest, determine what information can be shared to reduce the gossip, fear, and misinformation that will spread through your company if you do not communicate with your employees.
- Do you have an idea of what individuals or entire departments might be eliminated in a merger? We at WBENC have witnessed many mergers among our corporate members and see over and over again the stress and uncertainty faced by staff as the merger or acquisition progresses. If you are forming a partnership to achieve economies of scale, your staff will know this and will want to know how they fit into the picture. As stated above, it is a delicate balance to keep key staff on board and informed and protect your own and prospective partner's confidentiality.
- What about your industry's culture? Have you given thought to what the industry buzz will be? Are there publications or trade associations that could be a problem? Neutralizing any potential criticism should be part of the partnership strategy before it is announced. You may even be able to control the rhet-

oric describing the partnership, merger or acquisition with a professionally crafted press release that stresses the strengths of the partnership.

JUST-IN-TIME LEARNING: Impressing the Industry

Take a look at this (shortened) press release from corporate giants Kmart and Sears, Roebuck and Co. about how to position a merger, acquisition or partnership to your industry. Note the positive tone and attention to issues of interest to customers, shareholders, suppliers, vendors and other interested parties:

NEWS RELEASE

Kmart Holding Corporation and Sears, Roebuck and Co. Agree To Merge

TROY, Mich. & HOFFMAN ESTATES, Ill.—(BUSINESS WIRE)—Nov. 17, 2004—

Combination Creates 3rd Largest U.S. Retailer With $55 Billion in Annual Revenues; Will Have Broader Retail Presence and Improved Scale and Operational Efficiency

Kmart Holding Corporation and Sears, Roebuck and Co. announced today they have signed a definitive merger agreement that will combine Sears and Kmart into a major new retail company named Sears Holdings Corporation. Sears Holdings will be the nation's third largest retailer, with approximately $55 billion in annual revenues, 2,350 full-line and off-mall stores, and 1,100 specialty retail stores.

Both Sears, Roebuck and Kmart have made significant strides in transforming their organizations, and the merger will further accelerate this process for both companies. Sears Holdings will be headquartered in Hoffman Estates, IL, and Kmart will continue to have a significant presence in Troy, MI. **The combined business will have a broader retail presence and improved scale** through a national footprint of nearly 3,500 retail stores. The combined company will also benefit from **improved operational efficiency in areas such as procurement, marketing,**

information technology and supply chain management.

Under the terms of the agreement, which was unanimously approved by both companies' boards of directors, Kmart shareholders will receive one share of new Sears Holdings common stock for each Kmart share...

Edward S. Lampert, chairman of Kmart, will be the chairman of Sears Holdings. He will be joined in an Office of the Chairman by Alan J. Lacy, current chairman and chief executive officer of Sears, and Aylwin B. Lewis, current president and chief executive officer of Kmart...

Mr. Lampert said, "The combination of Kmart and Sears is extremely compelling for our customers, associates and shareholders as it will create a powerful leader in the retail industry, with greatly expanded points of distribution, leading proprietary home and apparel brands and significant opportunities for improved scale and operating efficiencies. The merger will enable us to manage the businesses of Sears and Kmart to produce a higher return than either company could achieve on its own."

...

Mr. Lacy said, "The combination will greatly strengthen both the Sears and Kmart franchises by accelerating the Sears off-mall growth strategy and enhancing the brand portfolio of both companies. This will clearly be **a win for both companies' customers while significantly enhancing value for all shareholders**. We will have a total combined store base of nearly 3,500 stores and the leading service organization in the industry capable of a major expansion to serve the needs of existing Kmart and Sears customers."

Sears Holdings will feature a powerful home appliance franchise as well as strong positions in tools, lawn and garden, home electronics, and automotive repair and maintenance. Key proprietary brands include Kenmore, Craftsman, and DieHard. The company will have a broad apparel offering, including such well-known labels as Lands' End, Jaclyn Smith, and Joe Boxer as well as the Apostrophe and Covington brands. It will also have Martha Stewart Everyday products, which are now offered exclusively in the U.S. by Kmart and in Canada by Sears Canada.

Kmart specialty retail stores will continue to carry their current lineup in proprietary home and fashion lines including Thalia Sodi, Jaclyn Smith, Joe Boxer, Martha Stewart Everyday, Route 66 and Sesame Street.

The combination of the two companies is conservatively estimated to generate $500 million of annualized cost and revenue synergies to be fully realized by the end of the third year after closing. The transaction, after giving effect to estimated synergies, is expected to be significantly accretive to earnings per share in the first year before one-time restructuring costs.

...

The company expects to achieve annual cost savings of over $300 million principally through improved merchandising and non-merchandising purchasing scale as well as improved supply chain, administrative and other operational efficiencies. In addition, the combined company will complete a full store asset review as part of a plan to monetize non-strategic real estate assets as appropriate.

...

The merger, which is expected to close by the end of March 2005, is subject to approval by Kmart and Sears shareholders, regulatory approvals and customary closing conditions. **Lehman Brothers served as financial advisor to Kmart, and Simpson Thacher & Bartlett LLP provided legal counsel to Kmart. Morgan Stanley served as financial advisor to Sears, and Wachtell, Lipton, Rosen & Katz provided legal counsel to Sears.**

SOURCE: Kmart Holding Corporation & Sears, Roebuck and Co.

Once you have given serious thought to all of the many timing issues surrounding any potential partnership situation, you will better be able to consider all of the possible partnership scenarios you can consider.

Not Quite Ready to Partner? Consider a Mentor-Protégé Relationship

What if your answer to "Is now the right time to consider a new partnership?" is a resounding "No!" or even a "Hmmm... I'm not exactly sure"? While your reason for hesitation may relate to a specific element of your business that needs to be addressed before you "put yourself out there" to potential partners, there may be other factors at work. If your uncertainty about partnership is due to uncertainty about your own leadership style, your readiness for growth or another "personal" factor, you may want to consider finding a business mentor to specifically work with you on partnership-related issues.

I am a firm believer in the importance of mentoring—a component of the "Support Networks" building block of partnerships. I have a few important mentors myself, and also serve as a mentor to several people, including my younger writing collaborator, Lindsey Pollak. (In fact, as we were writing this book, Lindsey was simultaneously entering into a partnership—with a new boyfriend. As she told me about introducing the new beau to her parents—"Meet the Parents," she joked, citing the popular Ben Stiller movies—I insisted that she set up a "Meet the Mentor" so I could check out the guy as well. I am happy to report that I approved of the partnership!)

Even if you are sure that a partnership is the right move for you, it helps to have a mentor serve as an advisor and friend during the process. This person may already serve as a mentor to you, or it may be someone new you seek out to help you through the process of forming and executing a new strategic alliance. Either way, I do recommend that you consult with someone "on your side," no matter what type of partnership(s) you choose to pursue.

When it comes to mentoring, there are both formal and informal mentor-protégé relationships. Before entering into either type of relationship, remember that a mentor-protégé relationship is yet another type of partnership, and must follow the "win-win-win" philosophy in order to be successful. Here are two examples of mentoring partnerships to help spur your thinking about seeking out a new mentor, or maximizing an existing mentor-protégé relationship.

First comes advice and inspiration from a Q and A with Bruce Perkins, Vice President and Manager, Supplier Diversity at Merrill Lynch, and a longtime WBENC supporter.

Q: How often do you mentor business owners?

A: I try to do mentoring whenever I can. It's my passion *and* part of my job.

Q: How do your protégés or "mentees" find you?

There is a certain amount of "formal" mentoring of vendors in our [Merrill Lynch] program, but for the most part I mentor people referred to me by other people I have mentored or other people I know—suppliers and other businesspeople. If someone comes and says, "I want you to mentor me, then that is a bond of trust. It is an honor."

Q: What is the first question you ask a business owner when you are mentoring her?

A: I think it is important not to go into a mentoring relationship with preconceived ideas about what is success. I start by asking the WBE how she defines success. It may be different from what is written in her business plan. I always want to find out what determines success for the women I mentor.

Q: Besides general business advice, what else can a corporate mentor offer to a WBE protégé?

A: I give mentees an opportunity to meet very successful women business owners by referring them to other people who exhibit excellence in what they do. I hope their successful practices will rub off on the mentees and it usually does.

Referrals are another big part of mentoring process. I have been in procurement for 35 years and supplier diversity for 15 years. Those of us in the business give each other quality referrals.

Finally, a key component of mentoring is education. Eighty percent of the educational sponsorships I have provided in the last three to four years have been to women. I send to them to the Tuck course [the Tuck-WBENC Executive Program, sponsored by IBM, a one-week intensive executive development program] and other programs at the University of Wisconsin at Madison and the Kellogg School of Business at Northwestern University.

PROFITABLE MENTORSHIP: Dougherty Sprague Environmental, Inc. and the Department of Defense's Mentor-Protégé (MP) Program

Another example of mentor-protégé partnership comes from WBE Cathy Dougherty. According to Cathy, a mentor-protégé program "saved our company and has provided great assistance as we grow!" Here is the story in her own words—note how her story demonstrates the length of time partnership development can take, and the importance of going with your gut when choosing the right partner, even for a mentoring relationship:

"Dougherty Sprague Environmental, Inc. (DSE) is a small, woman-owned environmental and engineering firm based in

Dallas, Texas. I founded the company in 1998. Almost immediately the private environmental market went south as business spent their bucks on Y2K and interest rates were rising. I decided we needed to use our woman-owned status to look at U.S. government contracting. Even after eight years' experience as a consultant with a large multi-national firm, I had no earthly idea of how to begin to market to the federal government. It was then that I became aware of the Department of Defense's Mentor Protégé program.

"MPs are special partnerships, usually sponsored by a government agency, and partner a large prime contractor with a small, usually disadvantaged firm. I researched the programs and found that every branch of the military, as well as NASA, has an MP program and they are all slightly different! SBA has its own, too. Some are funded; some are not. Some are for only one contract; some extend over multiple contracts. This makes the process quite confusing! At a trade show, I meet Geary Case, the Air Force Mentor Protégé Program Manager with the corporation Weston Solutions, San Antonio. Not only did he take the time to explain the different programs, but he also told me the Air Force program was my best choice for a number of reasons. Weston had a current protégé, but we began a dialogue that lasted for over a year.

In late 2000, we submitted our MP proposal to the Air Force, but were not funded. By this time, several other firms had also approached us, but I had questions for them (before becoming their protégé), and I did not like some of their answers (so did not form a relationship with them, still preferring Weston). In May 2001, the Air Force finally accepted our teaming proposal and Weston and DSE entered into a formal MP agreement.

"The terms of the MP agreement required multiple commitments from both of us:

- What we at DSE got: They were to help me with infrastructure issues, such as accounting, marketing, policy and management training. They had a former government auditor review our accounting system practices, help develop procedures, and teach me how to prepare pricing for IDIQ [Indefinite Delivery Indefinite Quantity] bids and make sure I would survive the audit. I attended an executive training seminar for a week and they helped us prepare numerous marketing brochures, government 254/255 forms and other marketing pieces. We even were allowed to attend trade shows and work out of their booth. They also had to transfer a technology to us. Weston provided training for our technical staff on topics of our choice, such as bioremediation and complex groundwater modeling. They even got us groundwater modeling software at a significant discount. (Unfortunately, there is no free ride: they cannot provide equipment for free or lend money.) I had to spend a lot of time on the relationship, and there was a significant amount of auditing and reporting.

- What they got: Weston received $200,000 for very specific reimbursements and program management, brownie points with the Air Force, a qualified and certified SDB [Small Disadvantaged Business] for their minority goals on contracts, and reduced purchasing time, as they did not have to get competitive bids on a project that was completed by their protégé. Plus, they certainly received my undying gratitude!

"While getting business is not the primary function of the MP program, developing the protégé into a viable prime government contractor is. So, we were allowed to partner or be a First Tier subcontractor on six Weston prime contracts for the Environmental Protection Agency, the Air Force, and the U.S. Postal Service. Our largest contract is the EPA Region VI START (Emergency Response). It took over seven months following our MP agreement to receive any government work at all though Weston. The first contract was a large asbestos and lead paint survey at Fort Sam Houston. Our performance on the first project was, at best, "fair." I ended up later firing the project manager and I thought the relationship was over! And I admit that just to be added as a subcontractor was sometimes an arduous process. And, we had to qualify as a Small Disadvantaged Business (SDB) with the SBA, which was another highly bureaucratic endeavor.

"Weston held my hand every step of the way and finally we were able to place a full-time person on the EPA START team in August 2001 (value: about $120,000 per year for four years). *Note: If you are keeping track, that is over 18 months since I said, "Hey, let's go get some government work!"* All other plans that we had made with Weston did not happen due to 9/11. No other federal work was awarded by Weston for six months except on a few small post office contracts. We limped through the remainder of our formal agreement without much work, due to no fault of Weston's.

"Then we answered the call on Saturday morning, February 1, 2002, that the Space Shuttle Columbia had just broken apart over East Texas. We helped Weston assist the EPA and NASA for the next four months in shuttle recovery efforts. This fall, we had personnel in Florida for over two months assisting the Army COE [Corps of Engineers] and FEMA on hurricane clean-up recovery—not working for Weston, but due to the shuttle work, working for another prime. In 2004, we received our 8(a) certification and a GSA environmental contract, and we are pushing on. *None of this would have been possible in such a short (in government terms) time frame without the MP program!*

"Our MP agreement with Weston has resulted in over $3.5 million dollars in sales and continues to bring credibility to our firm with other prime contractors. We continue to have ups and downs, but without Weston's MP program, we would have had to close our doors. The Weston MP program manager is the best and he has been supported by Weston management at every level. It has been a great partnership which we hope continues for many years!"

If you are interested in pursuing a formal mentor-protégé relationship, contact the government body that you are interested in targeting with your products or services. As Dougherty states, the purpose of the mentor-protégé relationship is to enhance the capabilities of the protégés; and to improve their ability to successfully compete for federal contracts. When MP relationships thrive, everyone wins.

About the Department of Defense (DoD) Mentor-Protégé Program:
The DoD Mentor-Protégé Program was enacted in 1990 (Public Law 101-510) under the direction of former Senator Sam Nunn and Secretary of Defense William Perry. This program was established to provide incentives for (major) DoD prime contractors (mentors) to help small disadvantaged businesses (SDBs), qualified organizations that employ the severely disabled, and woman-owned small businesses (protégés) develop technical and business capabilities. The goal of the program is to assist protégés to successfully compete for prime contract and subcontract awards. Successful Mentor-Protégé agreements provide a winning relationship for the protégé, the mentor and the DoD. Current participants include companies specializing in environmental remediation, engineering services and information technology, manufacturing, telecommunications, and health care. For more information, visit www.acq.osd.mil/sadbu/mentor_protege.

When the Timing is Right: Types of Partnerships to Consider

If you answer a resounding "YES!" to the question, "Is now the right time to partner?" your next step is to figure out what type of alliance to pursue. As you saw in Bain & Company's highly inclusive definition of strategic alliances in Chapter Two, there are numerous types of partnerships you can consider as you grow your business. I absolutely encourage you to consider all of your options: do not enter a particular type of partnership because it is the only one you understand. Believe me, there are as many different options as there are businesses to partner with—so be creative! Up until this point in the book I have used words like partnership, alliance and relationship interchangeably. While they often are, now it is time to get more specific.

JUST-IN-TIME LEARNING: Partnership is a Skill

"If you are new to business partnering, respect the learning curve and know that it may take you several years to master the art of partnering well. If you are a seasoned veteran of partnerships, you know from experience that the learning never ends when you are in partnership. Successful partnership centers on working in relationship with your partner, clients, employees and vendors, and requires endless personal growth and dedication to improvement. With every new partner, you will need to change some personal habits, tolerate differences in work style, accept criticism and give up some control. What worked for one partner might not work at all for your next. Partnering is a life-long course you never graduate from—if you choose to do it well. Partnering favorably is, however, a learnable skill that you can dedicate yourself to achieving."

- Azriela Jaffe, Let's Go Into Business Together: Eight Secrets to Successful Business Partnering, Career Press, 2001

David and Goliath: Strategic alliance with a large corporation

Let us assume in this scenario that you are the "David." The obvious pro of working with a "Goliath," a company much larger than your company or a partner with greater influence in your industry, is that you gain access to a larger playing field. That was certainly true for Cathy Dougherty when she partnered with Weston and gained access to federal government contracting opportunities. As a general rule (but not in all situations, of course), large companies have more people, more money, more equipment, farther reach and more robust technology. Partnering in a strategic alliance with a larger company can help you to serve larger customers, fulfill bigger contracts and build your reputation in your industry. Partnering with a more influential person, a "name brand," can open doors that provide increased opportunity.

Remember that even the world's largest corporations cannot do everything by themselves, so they rely on partnerships to fuel their own growth and customer satisfaction. If you fill a unique niche in your industry you are particularly well positioned to partner with a large corporation—even if you currently consider that company to be a competitor.

PROFITABLE PARTNERSHIP:
Pfizer's Managed Service Program

Some progressive corporations offer formal programs around their efforts to partner with GMEs. Pat Birmingham, Associate Director, Vendor Management, Pfizer Global Sourcing, shares information about their program:

"The Managed Service Program (MSP) that we have implemented is an extremely successful alliance with WMBEs that provides ample opportunity for WMBEs to provide contract resources to our company in a structured, competitive, yet fair manner. We currently have 56 classified WMBEs that have active contractors on our sites through the MSP relationship which accounts for 24.85 percent of the total contractor head count. Our service provider, who works with us to insure that the WMBE firms are in the program and that they receive opportunities to position contractors with us, tracks and trends the opportunities and exposure for us."

One program member is CCN, Inc., led by CEO and Chairman Clarice Kennedy. Her company's gross billings with Pfizer, in 2004, reached $2 million and she calls the MSP program a "true partnership effort."

"[Pfizer's] MSP is one of the best in the industry. It is extremely proficient, easy to use and offers vendors a fair opportunity to perform...Pfizer 'opened the door' to allow my company to succeed, however, we were not given special treatment just because we are woman-owned. Once the door was opened, it was up to us to prove ourselves and we did!"

According to Kathy Greco, Director of the supplier diversity program at the large staffing company Manpower Professional, "Working together is the only way we can all grow. In the past we all competed, but there is enough business for everyone and working together will bring us all new opportunities. We are all in this together."

Kathy also reminds small and GME business owners not to be intimidated by forming an alliance with a Goliath: "Remember that you are partnering with *people* (like me and members of my team) who are passionate – not just a corporation. Think of the partnership as teams working together – not just paper flowing back and forth."

Kathy and her team at Manpower truly practice what they preach. Several of their stories appear throughout this book, and one I find particularly exciting is Manpower's relationship with Superior Design International (SDI), a WBE and MBE niche technology staffing company owned by Carmen Castillo. Kathy and Carmen have not only become business partners, but also friends. Here is their story in their own words:

Kathy: I heard about Carmen from a corporate customer who suggested that I consider adding her organization to our supplier net-

work. I did my homework and looked her up! Carmen was presenting an award at an event in New York and Manpower had already purchased a table. I attended the event and just walked up and introduced myself. I continued to contact Carmen and began to discuss opportunities and ideas as we began to build a relationship and introduce our staffs to one another. We could instantly see how important this partnership would be.

Carmen: I felt honored. Manpower was our largest competitor. I knew we would be a good mix. It was in my best interest to work closely with Manpower. I knew they could take me to the next level. My customers were pleased, too. Everyone knows Manpower, so when we work together, customers do not feel like they are taking a chance with me.

All David-Goliath relationships do not function as smoothly as the relationship between Manpower and SDI. The major drawback to a David-Goliath alliance is the fact that the Goliath-sized business holds a lot of power. If you decide to partner with a much larger company, be careful that your alliance is not really an acquisition. Keep that important building block—strategic vision—top-of-mind. Remember that big companies usually have big legal teams, so get all of your alliance details in writing. Having your financial building block in place and up-to-date will provide you with key metrics for your own as well as your potential partner's analysis and will add to the image of your firm as you enter into discussions.

Another drawback to partnering with a big company is the likelihood that you may be working with a middle manager or even a junior staffer. Be sure you are comfortable with the people at the Goliath company—if that relationship is strong and positive, the alliance has a better chance of being mutually beneficial.

Even the largest of corporations have customers. In the supplier diversity world, second tier spend has become a standard and important factor in many bids and contract negotiations. You may view a prospective contract with an IBM as the prize of the decade for you and your company, but realize that they may also celebrate discovering a partner for their own marketing goals.

JUST-IN-TIME LEARNING:
When is an alliance really an acquisition?

If you take a look at our original list of what makes a successful marriage, and reverse the recommendations, you can get an idea of what would make a partnership fail or become an acquisition. Some examples:

- The partners are not kind to each other.
- The partners do not communicate.
- The partners do not allow themselves to be influenced by the other partner, or one partner dominates or manipulates the other.
- The partners no longer share the same dreams and goals.
- Conflicts are not resolved.
- Each partner feels some level of contempt for the other.

Remember that *your company* may be the Goliath in some situations, or you may be the one to consider turning a partnership into an acquisition. As WBE Pamela O'Rourke, CEO of Icon Information Consultants, likes to say, "If you can't beat 'em, buy 'em!"

Goliath and David: Working with a much smaller partner

No matter the size of your business, sometimes you are the Goliath and it can be advantageous to partner with a smaller company. One of the major benefits of partnering with a smaller business is that you often hold the leverage when negotiating. You may also find a stronger degree of loyalty and attentiveness from a smaller partner because your relationship is likely to bring them a significant amount of revenue. You are also much more likely to interact directly with the owner or senior staff of a smaller partner company.

One very important reason to partner with smaller firms is to increase your own supplier diversity spend. If you are fortunate enough to be a prime supplier to a corporation that counts its spend with women- and minority-owned suppliers, they will probably require that you report your second tier spend as well (see "Just-in-Time Learning," below). You get a marketing advantage with these firms when you can detail in a proposal the names and capabilities of the firms with which you partner.

How do you go about finding diverse suppliers for supplier alliances? You start by being accessible to new suppliers. You identify organizations and events where diverse suppliers participate and you become involved. You identify the areas of opportunities in your company and advertise the fact that you are seeking diverse suppliers in these commodities and services. You establish the criteria and capability requirements for diverse suppliers, which should include WBENC and/or NMSDC certification. You set your own internal goals and then decide what a good starting percentage of diversity spend would be. The automotive industry has challenged its suppliers to spend a minimum of 6 percent of their U.S. purchases with minority suppliers.

The National Women's Business Council (NWBC), on which I serve, is currently addressing the issue of the failure of the federal government to meet its 5 percent goal for woman-owned businesses. Marilyn Carlson Nelson, quoted above, is Chair of the NWBC. I have often heard her ask: When over 30 percent of U.S. businesses are 51 percent-or-more women-owned, shouldn't we consider five percent a floor rather than a goal?

As you begin to look for other GME businesses to fill your diversity spend goals, remember that you can purchase from other WBE firms smaller than your own (helping them to grow and observing their strengths and weaknesses), but they may also be able to purchase from you. Just as a corporation might want to start small with you to test your relationship, so can you evaluate the attributes of your suppliers and see if perhaps they could be utilized in a strategic alliance or whether it makes sense to acquire them to increase your company's size and scale.

WBENC's Access to Markets survey found that larger women's business enterprises receive more than half of their revenues from contracts with large corporations, while smaller woman-owned firms rely more heavily on revenues from small or medium businesses. Revenues from subcontracts and strategic alliances have become increasingly important over the past three years, with more than one quarter of revenues, on average, coming from such arrangements.

FAST FACTS

On average, 74 percent of woman business owners' current contracts with large corporations are as a first tier supplier and 22 percent are as a second tier supplier. Additionally, nearly half (45 percent) of respondents say that they have formed a joint venture or strategic alliance to jointly bid on a purchasing opportunity with a large corporation; on average, 5 percent of contracts with large corporations come from such strategic alliances or joint ventures.

- WBENC/Center for Women's Business Research Access to Markets Survey

WBE Nancy Connolly, CEO and Founder of Smart Page Technologies and Lasertone Corporation, is a major proponent of supplier diversity programs and actively seeks women and minority business partners. "Diversity programs are an integral part of who we are as a company," she says. "When we ask corporations to take a look at their diversity practices, we like to return, in kind, a mirror image of their diversity programs."

Nancy also shares advice on making sure a diversity program is successful. "When doing business with a large corporation though a supplier diversity program," she explains, "it is important to perform a thorough risk/benefit analysis of the contract, understand the likelihood of contract renewal and realistically define the impact on your business if the contract is not renewed. That being said, I fully support diversity programs among small minority- and woman-owned business. Sharing business with each other is a win-win for everyone. There just are not any downsides—assuming one understands the risks."

Opposite is a copy of Lasertone's information sheet on diversity:

Destination Diversity : Share the Business

WOMEN AND MINORITY-OWNED BUSINESSES CONTRIBUTE ENORMOUSLY TO THE ECONOMY. ACCORDING TO THE CENTER FOR WOMEN'S BUSINESS RESEARCH:

- ***Businesses owned by women or women of color increased 37% from 1997 to 2002.***
- ***We now number over 1 million businesses.***

Lasertone would like to take this opportunity to encourage everyone to **share the business.** We can leverage our record-growth and strength in numbers to help each other in a competitive market place – *just by doing business with one another.*

YOU'RE IN GOOD COMPANY

Lasertone, the nation's leading woman-owned manufacturer of networked printer supplies, services, and hardware was founded in 1989 by Nancy Connolly, President and CEO. Since then, the company has grown from a two-person, home-based operation to an industry leader with over 70 employees, state-of-the-art manufacturing facility, and national sales and distribution outlets.

WORKPLACE DIVERSITY

Lasertone supports workplace diversity because we understand it makes good business sense. Our commitment is reflected in our hiring practices — 60% of our employees are either minority or women. We celebrate the differences among our employees and benefit from the unique ideas a multicultural workforce brings to our business.

However, our dedication to diversity extends far beyond our workforce. We also incorporate diversity into business objectives and marketplace strategies. That commitment enhances our understanding of the business community and broadens our marketplace — *and that translates into more business.*

SUPPLIER DIVERSITY

A strong commitment to supplier diversity is a key component of our strategy. Supporting minority owned businesses adds value to the supply chain and enhances each participant's competitive position. We believe multicultural and women-owned businesses must **share the business** with each other to:

- ***Leverage buying power***
- ***Grow start-ups into thriving small businesses by supporting one another and sharing best practices.***

Our belief in **share the business** is a core value at Lasertone. We implemented a successful Supplier Diversity Program, resulting in a greater than 10% spend for the first quarter, 2004 with minority and women-owned suppliers. By tying diversity-marketing initiatives directly to our strategic business plan, we continue to develop new markets and share ideas with other women and minority-owned businesses.

STRATEGIC ALLIANCES

An integrated diversity program also means developing strategic alliances with other minority and women-owned businesses. When we partner with other businesses we can respond more effectively to competitive bid situations where singly, our businesses may not have the scope to compete and win.

SHARE THE BUSINESS; REAP THE REWARDS

If we **share the business** we will reap the rewards.
Doing business with each other helps us all increase our sales, develop new markets and increase our competitive advantage. Our businesses will become stronger, more competitive, and more profitable, if we **share the business.**

CONTACT INFORMATION

diversity@lasertone.com OR *www.lasertone.com*
265 Foster Street • Littleton, MA 01460 • 800-660-3855

lasertone
Network Printing Solutions

JUST-IN-TIME LEARNING:
Tiers Are Not Just on a Wedding Cake

When considering partnership possibilities with Davids and Goliaths alike, look to opportunities both up and down the corporate purchasing process. Here is an explanation of the tiers of a supply chain:

Second tier suppliers are diverse suppliers used as subcontractors by a first tier (also known as a prime) supplier to a corporation. Second tier suppliers generally count toward a company's supplier diversity goals, so it is in a corporation's best interest to ensure that their larger first tier suppliers meet and do business with smaller second tier players, and the first tier suppliers report on their usage of diverse subcontractors. Second tier supplying is yet another door into a corporation, and one that GMEs are increasingly using. In some cases you may be the first tier supplier, and in other cases you may be the second, third or fourth.

Why are second tier programs important to corporations and GMEs? As Rutgers University states on its procurement web site, "Second Tier sourcing programs have value because, by supporting the growth of minority- and woman-owned business on all levels of the economic food chain, they enhance the economic viability of all business concerns.

"The overall objective is to encourage the development and implement sustainable opportunities for [GMEs] to participate in the customer's procurement processes where it makes economic sense to do so.ii

Many of America's large corporations highly value second tier suppliers. They may be second tier, but they are by no means second-class.

- Excerpted from Breaking Through: Creating Opportunities for America's Women and Minority Owned Business by Susan Phillips Bari, 2004.

PROFITABLE PARTNERSHIP:
The Elements Inc. and Majority Businesses

The Elements Inc., a WBE firm owned by Debbie Faraone, provides specialty gifts and premiums. This is an intensely competitive business, especially in the women and minority business arena. Low cost of entry has allowed the creation of many companies but the demands of strategic sourcing efficiencies are now squeezing out many businesses that were once primes to large companies. Debbie understands the building blocks of timing and strategic vision. She recognized, after 9/11, that the downturn in her sales might never come back in the same manner as before, and she had to find a new niche in the supply chain of the future.

As a growth strategy, Faraone decided the answer was to reposition her firm in the supply chain and to directly design and manufacture some of the products she used to purchase for resale. This strategy allows her to serve as a second tier supplier for larger, majority-owned ad specialty companies that used to be her competitors and can now count their spend with her firm. By partnering in this way, Faraone is able to participate in large contracts where she has become a value-added partner rather than a competitor, and to increase her competitive stance as a prime on smaller contracts as well.

The Elements, which used to purchase the same products from manufacturers here and abroad, is now designing and manufacturing its own line of leather business accessories and writing instruments. Now that they have become a direct manufacturer with increased ability to adjust product to customer specifications, their quality and pricing are more attractive to their customer, and they can be more competitive in the supply chain.

According to Faraone, "By designing and manufacturing our own line, we will now be able to market ourselves to corporations and their contracted vendors, who are often not minority- or woman-owned, as a second tier supplier. Corporations often cannot choose a woman- or minority-owned business to support their ad specialty and premium needs due to their size and volume requirements. The large ad specialty companies that often receive these contracts are then required by the corporations to meet various standards and diversity goals in order to maintain that contract. Now, The Elements can help these companies meet their diversity goals as a second tier provider offering high quality leather business accessories, which include brief bags, pad folios and jotters, as well as quality writing instruments. For the hotel industry, we manufacture in-room directories, desk blotters, TV guide covers, menu covers and check covers.

"For those companies that are minority- or woman-owned, we can also support their diversity goals by providing them high quality leather accessories and writing instruments for their own corporate use or as a product they can resell."

Debbie Faraone certainly understands the importance of a "win-win-win" philosophy.

As with many things, the pros of a Goliath-David partnership also hint at the potential cons. Working with a smaller company always includes the risk that they rely so much on your business that they will not stay afloat without you, and may even go out of business during a period when your alliance is not drawing revenues for them. (This is the reason many supplier diversity executives like to recommend their suppliers to other corporations—so a vendor's eggs are not all in their basket.)

Working with a smaller alliance partner also means you run the risk of outgrowing them—by winning larger contracts that they cannot help you to fulfill. When working with a David partner, be particularly careful to get all expectations in writing, and be sure that you are aware of the capabilities and limitations of the smaller partner. Do they have their building blocks on a solid footing? Sound familiar? This is the same due diligence that the Goliaths do when considering *your* capabilities as a supplier.

Merger: Forming a new company from two formerly separate companies

Deciding to merge with another company has many ramifications, both personal and professional. Some of the greatest triumphs and greatest failures in the business world involve mergers. When should you even consider a merger with another company? Keith Hines advises businesses that have been in an alliance for more than five years to seriously consider a merger. "In the business cycle," he explains, "contracts generally run in three-to-five year periods. If you are in more than one contract cycle as an alliance, then you have synergy and you should take a closer look at your situation. You would be even more profitable if you merge. If you are already working that closely together and are running different systems, it is not efficient to be running those systems parallel to one another."

Acquisition: Forming a new company by one company's buying another company

"Though it can seem exciting and sexy, growth by acquisition is filled with booby traps and mine fields—particularly for the inexperienced," write Larry Fox and Rob Hilliard in their newsletter, *The CEO Refresher.* "Simply having the money to buy a company does not, in itself, assure success. Securing capital for an acquisition from your bank or through investors does not assure success. Receiving blessings from your most important customers does not assure success. Obtaining the enthusiastic support of your management team does not assure success."

So, what is their advice to entrepreneurs considering an acquisition? They offer three key success factors:

"The three factors that have the greatest impact on the success or failure of a business acquisition are: (1) having a thorough understanding of the acquisition target prior to closing the transaction, so there are no surprises after the ink is dry on the deal; (2) developing a post-closing plan that offers maximum potential to effectively integrate, operate and grow the acquired company in a post-transaction environment, and (3) executing that post-closing plan, which can be difficult and is highly dependent on how employees of the acquired company not only accept but proactively participate in the plan."*

If you are considering an acquisition—or being acquired—be sure to solicit expert advice on the complex legal, financial and human resource issues surrounding this type of transaction.

PROFITABLE PARTNERSHIP:
SBC Communications Offers a Corporate Perspective on Alliances, Mergers and Acquisitions

SBC Communications is at the vanguard of promoting partnerships and alliances as a strategy for the growth of diversity suppliers. The formal encouragement of alliances between its largest prime suppliers and smaller woman- and minority-owned businesses began in 1989 with the formation of SBC's Supplier Diversity Prime Supplier Participation Program. One of the first fruits of this effort was the development of the first woman-owned cable cutting business in the telecommunications industry, Complas. Originally a partnership between two women owners, Complas took over the entire cable cutting business for SBC regional affiliate, Pacific Bell, in 1992. Monica Garcia became the sole owner of Complas in 1994 and ran a highly successful business until 2000, when Complas was forced to close its doors during the telecom downturn.

* "Business Acquisition, Integration & Operation…and Communications 101: A Primer," by Larry Fox and Rob Hilliard, The CEO Refresher newsletter, 2005. http://www.refresher.com/!lfrhprimer.html

In the late 1990s, Cable Connection & Supply, owned by Barbara Vinar and based out of Faribault, Minnesota, was introduced by SBC to 3M and Tyco, the manufacturers of two products that SBC used in new telephone line installation. The three companies developed a solution where Cable Connection would provide value-added service by installing a Tyco block into a 3M closure and then distributing the product to SBC Midwest. This service decreased the cost of getting the product to SBC and cut the SBC technician's installation time in half.

More recently, SBC has found a very creative way to grow its relationship with WBENC-certified Rose International, owned by Himanshu Bhatia (see this company's own Profitable Partnership profile later this in this chapter). Rose has been providing temporary IT staff to SBC since 1999, growing its reach from Rose's St. Louis headquarters to providing staff augmentation across SBC's footprint. In 2004, Rose licensed SBC's internally developed vendor management system, enhanced and expanded its capabilities, and now markets this software system to corporations across the country as MaestroVMS.

Vertical Alliance: Partnering with other companies performing related services in your industry or serving your client base.

Vertical alliances can increase business for all partners involved—through referrals or bundled contracts that the alliance can bid for as a group.

For instance, WBE Betsy Mordecai, President and self-described "Queen of Quite-A-Lot" of MorSports & Events, Inc., a special events and meeting planning company based in Denver, Colorado, has a strategic alliance with International Management Group (IMG), the largest sports marketing firm in the world. Specifically, MorSports has worked on several programs with

IMG's Olympics consulting company, Disson & Associates, which handles marketing and Olympics sponsorships for the most prestigious Olympics sponsors. "We help them manage their clients' hospitality programs," Betsy explains. "They do not want to make this part of their core capability, but they want a team to call on when a client needs this aspect of their program handled. We have handled Korbel's and Kleenex's Olympics programs through Disson & Associates, along with many other programs. We have had a relationship since the inception of our company."

In another mutually beneficial alliance relationship, MorSports partnered with Newks Group, a sports marketing firm in Sydney, Australia, owned by famous tennis player, John Newcombe. According to Betsy, Newks Group "had many clients that they handled for overall events and many of their clients approached them about Olympic programs. They had the inside knowledge in Sydney, but not the Olympic experience. We formed a team to handle all of their Olympic groups, handling over 6,000 people in Sydney during the 2000 Olympic Games."

Thanks to such important and successful alliances, and her company's own track record of achievement, Betsy and her team are currently preparing for the next Olympic Games in Turin, Italy, and Beijing, China!

What are some of the drawbacks of a vertical alliance? For one, the situation may ebb and flow business-wise, depending on what particular area of business each partner is servicing. There are no guarantees that every client will need or even want the services of both (or all, if there are multiple) partners.

PROFITABLE PARTNERSHIP:
EAP Lifestyle Management, LLC

WBE Patricia Vanderpool's company, EAP Lifestyle Management, LLC, is built on win-win-win partnerships. "It is through our relationships with other businesses that we are able to grow and to expand our services," she says. As you will see from her detailed story, EAP Lifestyle Management benefits from a wide variety of partnerships with small businesses, nonprofit organizations, large corporations and sole proprietors—all with the goal of serving their shared client base.

"It wasn't long after purchasing EAP Lifestyle Management that I saw a need for us to expand our menu of services. For our business to survive and to thrive, we had to have resources to meet our clients' needs.

"EAP Lifestyle Management offers employee assistance program and work/life services on a national level, with international expansion planned. We offer assistance, resources and support to both employees and management for any problem or issue they may have. As we hear from our client companies and survey the market, we expand our services by working with other organizations to provide services the employee or manager may request.

"EAP Lifestyle Management began providing only family and individual counseling services for employees of about ten local businesses. When I realized we would need to offer expanded employee assistance program and work/life services, I began to partner with other businesses.

"One of the first requests we received from a large client company was to provide outplacement services to support their downsizing efforts. We developed a plan to deliver services, including support, by having mental health and EAP counselors on-site. Anticipating the needs of employees who were to be downsized, we offered résumé skill development, printing of résumés, resources such as links to employment agencies and to financial institutions, interview skill development, and networking opportunities. We were able to provide these services through relationships with local businesses. I have also developed partnerships with staffing agencies. As is the usual procedure for staffing companies, there is no fee to the employee. This enables me to offer this piece of our outplacement services at no additional cost to me or to my client companies.

EAP Lifestyle Management then expanded to offer financial assessment and referral services. Again, we were able to do this by aligning ourselves with financial agencies and institutions. We have partnered with Consolidated Credit Counseling, a non-profit debt consolidation company, that has withstood the criticism in that field and achieved much growth and recognition themselves. I was first introduced to Consolidated Credit by a visit from their account representative. He so impressed our office staff that we scheduled additional meetings. I began working with them within a year after purchasing EAP Lifestyle Management and continue to enjoy an excellent working relationship with them today. Consolidated Credit provides us, at no charge, a specially designated toll-free number and web access, so we can track utilization for the companies we serve. They also provide us a link on our web site and workplace posters and coupons for each employee. All this is at no charge to us. We are then able to offer this service to our client companies, their management, employees and their family members.

"We have recently forged a relationship with Primerica Financial Services to provide expanded financial services for our clients. Primerica will offer financial consultations and education at no cost to us or to our client company employees and their family members. They will provide us with announcements of their services and they will also provide workplace seminars at no charge to us or to our clients, which we can then offer to our client companies, their management, employees and their family members.

"We, while following up on a referral from Consolidated Credit Services, spoke with a small business owner who provided assistance to families in danger of losing their homes to foreclosure. Homesavers, Inc. provides us with workplace posters and initial consultations at no charge to our clients or to us, yet another service we can offer to our client companies.

"In another partnership, working with the U.S. Army Corps of Engineers, we were asked to provide a CD presentation as part of their Welcome Home project for employees returning from Iraq and for their families. The Corps of Engineers paid all production costs. Several months later, when I was asked by a company I serve to provide web-based alcohol and drug awareness and supervisor training, I was able to contact the person responsible for the production of the Welcome Home CD to get assistance in producing web-based training at a reasonable cost.

"For many years, I have been the mental health consultant and EAP provider for the Poarch Creek Indian reservation in Atmore, Alabama. They have come to be my family, and I have learned so much, personally and professionally, from them. I am culturally enriched because of my relationship with the tribe. Poarch Creek Indian Enterprises operates gaming facilities in north Alabama, just outside of Montgomery. They requested that we provide EAP services for their employees. Because they wanted our regular on-site presence, they provided us with local office space, at no cost to us! They are now experiencing tremendous growth and are working with Harrah's to upgrade their gaming facilities. They provided me with an introduction to Harrah's, who was very encouraging about the possibilities of working together when the new facility is built.

"Being a WBENC-certified woman-owned business has opened up a world of possibilities for us, paving the way for mutually rewarding relationships with other woman-owned businesses. The WBENC affiliation has helped connect us with potential clients.

"Without the continued support of our "partners," or without the alliances we have formed, EAP Lifestyle Management would be unable to meet the needs of our covered employees and their family members. We look forward to a future of new and continued relationships with other businesses and agencies to meet the needs of our clients.

Horizontal Alliance: Partnering with other companies that share the same product or service

Companies can serve a larger client base by expanding capacity or geographic reach. Note that a horizontal partnership may, by necessity, involve partnering with competitors. Some companies are not comfortable working with or sharing information and marketing opportunities with competitors, so you will have to decide if this option can work for you.

PROFITABLE PARTNERSHIP: WE Print

When Carol Louis, President, Louis Companies, wanted to spur growth for her firm, she developed two key strategies. First, she expanded her Arlington, Texas, company's offerings from traditional commercial printing to complete outsourced solutions for document distribution, fulfillment and inventory management. Today, the company serves as a one-stop shop for everything from stationery and business forms to labels, promotional products and more.

Next, Carol decided to create a base of strong alliances with businesses and organizations that could share leads, expertise and encouragement.

She chose to work with WBENC and its local affiliate, the Women's Business Council – Southwest (WBCS). Both groups provided excellent networking opportunities, in addition to mentoring relationships.

While attending WBENC meetings, Carol met executives from other woman-owned printing firms all around the nation. She had a brainstorm—what if these companies could create a printing alliance? Collectively, they could handle large contracts and compete with bigger companies.

So Carol founded WE Print, which now has six members. Working together, the group places bids for massive printing contracts with Fortune 500 companies—something no single member could do on its own.

Through WBCS, Carol met fellow board member Bruce Perkins, an executive with Merrill Lynch. Bruce agreed to mentor Carol, helping her build and market WE Print. Another mentor, Len Greenhalgh, Ph.D., professor of management at the Tuck School of Business at Dartmouth College, also agreed to coach Carol as she pursued large-scale contracts. Yet another, Connie Magers at JC Penney, provided ongoing support as Carol developed WE Print.

"By working together, our group can pursue business opportunities that will allow each and every one of our businesses to grow exponentially," Carol said. "And to do this, we've tapped into advisors who are willing to provide expertise and support. They simply want to see us succeed. And with their help, we will."

JUST-IN-TIME LEARNING: Never bad-mouth the competition...you may regret it later!

While it is often good business practice to feel a sense of competitive spirit, be careful how you talk about your competitors to potential corporate customers. As you will see in several stories in this book, past competitors can become future alliance partners! Here is some wise advice on the subject from Carol Danoff of Pitney Bowes:

"Never undermine the competition, EVER. Never claim that you are better than someone else at their expense. I would tend to promote the things that you do well and not bad-mouth someone else or say that you can do it better than them. Most folks in sourcing feel you should stand on your own merit, which means you should not have to bad-mouth. Especially if you end up partnering with them later!"

Sole to Sole

Many certified businesses consist of a single person working for himself or herself. Alliances and collaborations among sole proprietors such as consultants, writers, speakers and coaches can lead to big profits all around.

Professional speaker Julia Hubbel, President of The Hubbel Group in Lakewood, Colorado, offers insight into one of her successful sole-to-sole partnerships:

"I have just approached a talented young author for collaboration. His book is a best seller and is taking him on overseas assignments and speaking engagements. However, he is not a trained speaker. Our work overlaps perfectly. I am helping him develop his product line and speaking skills while including him on consulting projects. Conversely, he is likely to bring me to his clients. Because of doing some projects together, we are likely to work on a book based on those projects. There is a perfect complement and we both gain from the arrangement."

Hiring a Partner

In some instances, you may like a person (a business owner or executive) so much that you invite that person to become a partner in your existing company. As you will see in some of the stories included in this book, such as those about Roz Alford and Nancy Williams of ASAP Staffing or Jodi Clausman and Kelly Hess of Global Legal Services, sometimes a business owner can benefit from a sharing of leadership responsibilities.

PROFITABLE PARTNERSHIP: ASAP Staffing

One of the most successful WBE partnerships I know of, ASAP Staffing, was formed because one of the company's partners was involved in an acquisition. Nancy Williams, now Co-President of ASAP Staffing, explains, "Mergers and acquisitions are very hard on internal employees. Unless you are on the acquisition side, as an employee you are not going to have the upper hand and may not even have a job. So, during the acquisition [of my former employer] I was looking around and thinking about starting my own business."

At the same time that Nancy was getting fed up with serial acquisitions, Roz Alford was sensing that the time had come for her company, ASAP Staffing, to make some changes as well. Nancy recalls, "My husband actually worked for ASAP and heard the rumors that it was up for sale. I thought, I will approach Roz and see if she is interested in selling to Brannon and Tully [Nancy's employer at the time], so we met for lunch."

According to Roz, "[ASAP was] doing great and our size moved up to about 120 employees. We were not yet quite big enough to become a prime, but we had all these second tier relationships and were being approached regularly by other IT staffing firms that wanted to buy my company. I did not want to sell...I had worked with Nancy in a client relationship, seen her in action, and thought she filled the bill." At the time, Nancy was 33 and Roz was 49.

According to Nancy, she and Roz "courted" for six months and formalized their partnership in January 1998. Coincidentally, their official "marriage" occurred the day before Roz's wedding anniversary!

How did this partnership lead to greater business opportunities for the new firm? Once the partnership deal was sealed, Nancy called her former Brannon and Tully client, BellSouth, to tell them about her move to ASAP as a partner. Her BellSouth contact's comments were flattering and he encouraged Nancy to come in to discuss the new "marriage."

Additionally, Nancy explains, "Accenture was just about to start their engagement with BellSouth. We got a positive response from them as well. The fact that I knew and had dealt with their executives was a big plus. They told us that they thought there would be a future opportunity. And then, within a year, we were able to become a prime supplier to BellSouth through a proper RFI and RFP process. We were also able to achieve a prime vendor relationship with Accenture during that first year."

Franchising—Franchisee or Franchisor?

One of the major advantages of entering into a franchise agreement is the support—financial, marketing, supplies, etc.—that the franchisee receives from the franchisor. However, it can be expensive to buy into a franchise, and many entrepreneurs do not like to give up individual control of their company to the franchisor. However, there are also benefits that GME firms may find by becoming the franchisor.

Marilyn Carlson Nelson, CEO of Minneapolis-based Carlson Companies, a family-owned business, views franchising through a different lens. Several Carlson Companies divisions—Radisson Hotels, TGI Friday's and Carlson Wagonlit Travel—are franchise businesses. Marilyn views her franchisees as her partners that provide the equity capital to grow the brand. "As a private company, my Dad recognized early on that we would always would be short of capital and needed rigor around management of capital," she says. "This drove the concept of franchising—a kind of partnership. We still franchise in hotels, restaurants and travel agencies, where the most efficient use of money was marketing, business models and aggregating. We could grow with franchisees as partners, especially in international restaurants where [our franchisees] brought domestic knowledge, human resources, marketplace (consumers) and we brought business models and improved probabilty of their success. This was key to our being the first casual dining company to be truly international.

"The same thing has happened in our hotel and travel franchises. From the franchisee point of view, it is hard for individual owners of hotels and travel agencies to compete in today's high-tech, low-margin world. By becoming franchisees, they have access to management techniques, connectivity and technology and can increase their voice. For instance, by partnering in this way we have a bigger voice to lobby for issues like health care."

PROFITABLE PARTNERSHIP: Carlson Companies

The history of Carlson Companies is one of the classic business success stories in the American free enterprise system. Starting in 1938 with an idea and a $55 loan, entrepreneur Curtis L. Carlson (1914-1999) founded the Gold Bond Stamp Company in his home city of Minneapolis. Carlson knew that grocery stores, drug stores, gas stations and other independent merchants could use trading stamps, which could be redeemed for merchandise, to distinguish themselves from their competitors. During the 1950s and 1960s, in fact, Gold Bond and sister company, Top Value Stamps, helped revolutionize the way retail goods were marketed. Trading stamps proved to be right for the times and swept the nation in a wave of dramatic growth.

In the late 1960s, when the trading stamp market reached its peak, the Gold Bond Stamp Company expanded into the hospitality industry. In the 1970s, the company acquired dozens of additional businesses, including the highly successful T.G.I. Friday's restaurant chain and internationally renowned Ask Mr. Foster travel agencies. To reflect its diversification, Gold Bond changed its name to Carlson Companies in 1973.

Curtis' daughter, Marilyn Carlson Nelson, became CEO of the company in 1998, after holding virtually every executive job, including COO. According to Marilyn, one of the country's leading women business owners, smart, careful partnership is her strategy for leading her family business into the future:

"Our growth strategy has been partnership," she says. "At Carlson, our goal is to keep the core private and have it endure for several generations. We are careful that we do not enter into any partnership that will endanger the whole. Sometimes you are not negotiating from strength and you just have to acknowledge that. Sometimes, you do the best you can and then you have to decide if the partnership is valuable if someone else is in control. Sometimes you have to take that risk to survive, grow or enter a new market."

Cause-Related Alliance

Remember the fifth building block of partnership, strategic vision. If your corporate vision involves giving back to your community, a cause-related alliance may be an excellent option for you to achieve your long-term goals. Cause-related partnerships, often with a marketing focus, also provide many benefits in terms of branding and public relations. There can be strong business benefits in collaborating with a charity, school or other good cause. However, most nonprofit organizations work with tight budgets. This means they may be understaffed and/or have little leeway in negotiating partnership terms. Many major corporations have developed "affinity relationships" with the nonprofits they support, and that strategy to enter niche markets is now being emulated by smaller firms.

Partnerships without Borders

Keith Hines likes to say that going global is like buying a large house: "Make sure you are well-financed, have good advice and a little extra money, and be patient." Wise advice, indeed. There is a lot of money to be *made* by partnering overseas, there is a lot of money to be *saved* by partnering overseas, and there are a lot of headaches and risks that come with partnering overseas.

Hines also wisely points out that, "International partnership is the next wave. Increasingly, foreign companies are growing and looking for domestic partners, and vice versa." But the challenges cannot be underestimated: cultural differences can be harder to navigate than one might think, as can international laws, regulations, tariffs and other matters. "International partnership is difficult, but not impossible," Hines continues. "It is definitely not for the squeamish or those living month-to-month. It is the way to go if you *really, really* want your business to grow."

PROFITABLE PARTNERSHIP: Rose International

WBE Himanshu Bhatia, CEO of St. Louis-based Rose International, an IT services provider, is heavily involved in global partnerships. We asked for her expert advice based on her experience partnering across borders:

Q: With what international alliances are you currently involved?
A: We are working with other international businesses here in the U.S. to enhance the opportunities for women entrepreneurs in countries around the world. The U.S. clearly leads the world in recognition of the talent and abilities of its women business leaders. In 2004, Rose partnered with IBM, the Turkish Ministry of Industry and others to sponsor an International Forum on Women's Entrepreneurship in Istanbul, Turkey. We look forward to maintaining the momentum with such partners to help women in business worldwide.
From the perspective of a contracted business alliance, we have a strong relationship with our subsidiary, Rose IT Solutions, LLC (RITS), which is an India-based company. It is important for U.S. companies of every size to develop partnerships with companies that can provide support services synergistic with the delivery of their main product or service. While RITS has proven itself a formidable force in software and business service delivery, we can't afford to rely solely on them. Our customers expect us to deliver as and when required. Therefore, we have contingency arrangements in place with other high quality companies that are ready to perform for Rose if needed.

Q: What makes your alliances successful?
A: Of first importance is picking the right partner. We held extensive discussions with our prospective partners about serving in contingency roles. Next, we were very clear in describing to them what the roles, responsibilities and expectations would be—before we ever engaged in contract term discussion. All parties must be very transparent in their dealings and expectations. Only then will they be able to make a good decision about whether or not to engage. It's best that a party walks away as soon as possible if the partnership is not of interest. Constant and regular communication is key to the success of any alliance. We meet weekly with all partners with an open agenda.

Q: What advice do you have for WBEs considering international alliances?
A: Talk with your customers that have an international presence. Inquire about bringing your services to those countries. The businesspeople in each country will know who your competitors are and which ones are worthy allies. Be prepared to travel. A carefully planned and qualified five-day trip can provide more insight than six months of phone calls.

Q: What other advice can you offer on alliances and partnerships?
A: Outside of performing due diligence and fully qualifying your prospective partner, I can't stress enough the importance of full disclosure regarding your intent and expectation. An international alliance requires significant energy. This is no time to make promises of what might be possible. Be a realist and let them know clearly what you want out of the relationship and what they can expect from you. Urge them to move forward only if they recognize your proposed alliance as an important piece in their business mix.

Former Clients or Vendors

Partnering with a former (or current) vendor or client can fit into any of the above-mentioned categories, but the situation does pose unique challenges and opportunities. The clear pro in this situation is that you are dealing with a known quantity; when you have worked with someone before, you know what to expect. Sometimes, though, it can be hard to break out of old habits, relationships, pricing structures, etc. If your business has changed significantly and/or you are now on the other side of the table from where you once sat, it may take some time to forge a new relationship based on these different dynamics. Are you willing to be flexible and change some of your current practices to provide a seamless integration with your partner?

When WBENC was created in 1997, there were four women's organizations that were providing WBE certification in their local markets (Women's Business Development Center/Chicago, Women's Business Council of Louisiana, the North Texas Women's Business Council and the Ohio Women's Business Development Center). While each of these organizations conducted certification that was similar in process and standards to those used by the NMSDC and its local councils to certify MBEs, there were some subtle and not so subtle differences. To provide a greater benefit to each of their client bases (both corporate and WBE) by providing what would now be a nationally accepted and respected certification, they had to compromise. Just as in a romantic relationship, communication was the first critical step. Once common values and goals were agreed upon, experience and expertise were brought to the forefront and each member of the alliance agreed to give up a little control and change their processes a little bit, in order to create a much greater good for all of them.

PROFITABLE PARTNERSHIP: McColl Garella, LLC

This is the story of the partnership between Hugh McColl, Jr. and Julie A. Garella. This partnership is profitable for the partners and for their clients—women business owners interested in a merger or acquisition:

During his long and prosperous banking career, WBENC Applause Award recipient Hugh McColl made a name for himself by conquering untapped markets.

Now, as co-founder of investment banking firm McColl Garella, LLC, the retired Bank of America CEO has a different target in his scope: middle-market female business owners in need of advice on mergers and acquisitions, and other investment services.

"This is a market that has been underserved or not served at all," said McColl, who also runs another investment banking firm, McColl Partners LLC, which provides similar types of services to middle-market businesses. McColl Garella focuses on a specific kind of client: the female business owner, chief executive officer or chief financial officer at a mid-sized company with annual revenues of $10 million to $300 million.

According to Sharon Hadary, Executive Director of the Center for Women's Business Research in Washington, DC, women-owned businesses with 100 employees or more are growing 68 percent faster than all businesses of similar size. That kind of growth means these businesswomen need trustworthy investment advice.

"McColl and Garella are doing this because they saw a business opportunity. This is not a social service. He and Julie ran the numbers and they have been the first movers in this market," stated Dr. Hadary. "They would not be getting into the business that they are if there was not the demand there," she said.

Ms. Garella joined McColl Partners in the beginning of 2002, and pitched the idea of a separate firm aimed at women after noticing few clients were female. Some of the firm's partners told

McColl they felt she didn't have enough experience, although Garella had also co-founded Carnegie Capital Advisors, the only investment advisory firm in the Carolinas owned by a woman.

"She told me she would work for nothing and earn only from the new business she brought to the firm," said McColl, who was impressed by her ambition. He said they began to talk and Garella convinced him there was a niche market that was not getting enough attention.

"No women were coming through (the doors of McColl Partners)," Garella said. "I knew that women-owned companies were the fastest-growing segment of the economy."

McColl did some research and came away with a new respect for women who own and run their own companies.

"They are very conservative in the way they have to manage money," he said. "And, despite the difficulties many companies are facing, these firms are in better shape than most because they are not leveraged. So there is not a lot of debt."

McColl brings his wisdom and a reputation for candor to McColl Garella. "I am not going to sugarcoat my advice to anyone," he said. "To be successful, we need to be straightforward.

"Capital lacks prejudice. It can only flow where opportunity exists and the only void here is knowledge."

McColl Garella advises clients on potential acquisitions or mergers, raising private equity or restructuring debt. The firm also offers direction on exit strategies, depending on an owner's goals.

"Buying or selling a business can be overwhelming," said Garella. "It is extremely important to seek guidance from the right people who fully understand how to steer the process and deliver results.

"Of course, Hugh McColl, with over 100 acquisitions under his belt, has brought exceptional experience to the company," she said.

Hadary said the retired banker's respect in the financial

community has opened doors that in the past might have been wedged shut to McColl Garella's potential customers.

"His backing is extremely powerful and I think they are well-positioned. Julie knows how to leverage his connections and his presence."

McColl would rather give the credit to his partner. "Julie is the mother of this company," he said. "It is 100 percent her idea. I happened to like her idea."

Julie owns 51 percent of the company, which is WBENC certified, and is the managing partner of the firm.

Putting a Name and Face to Your Partner Type

Now that you have an understanding of the building blocks of partnership and some of the many types of partnerships that exist, it is time to find the companies and individuals who fill the bill. The next step in the partnership process involves finding your perfect match.

Chapter Four

Matchmaker, Matchmaker... Finding the Right Match

It is one thing to decide what type of partnership matches up with your strategic vision; it can be quite another to find a real live person or company to fill the bill. Sometimes you will pursue a partnership because you have a particular partner in mind; at other times, you will need to find the right company or product to enhance your and your company's needs as defined in that strategic vision. (We will focus on the latter situation.) You may even be looking for that "dowry" to help you expand or to upgrade your technology. A clear understanding of each of the building blocks is important as you look at evaluating the match.

While the advice and research presented in this book can help guide you in the right direction, I am a strong believer in studying successful partnerships in order to learn the most valuable lessons. This chapter features several detailed success stories about business partners working together in a variety of ways; as you have seen in earlier chapters, I call them Profitable Partnerships. While this chapter focuses on finding the right match (the mutual attraction phase, to continue our marriage analogy), Chapter Five brings you to the table with that potential match—the living, breathing person—for the essential process of negotiating a real partnership plan (the courtship or dating phase).

Preparing for Divorce

What? Was I not just talking about finding the perfect partner and reading lots of inspiring success stories? Yes, but as much as I am a romantic, I am also a realist. The very first day I went to work at the American Woman's Economic Development Corporation (AWED) in 1990, I sat in on a counseling session with a new woman business owner. The company she was soon to start happened to be a partnership. The very first question the AWED business counselor asked her was:

"How do you want your partnership to end?"

She looked somewhat bewildered, so the counselor continued, "Will your partnership go on indefinitely? Would you consider a buy-out or being bought out? Will you go public? Do you want to pass your share to your children? What about your partner's children—do you want to work with them? Will you eventually sell your company?

"You have to think about this at the beginning," the counselor said, "so that every contingency is addressed in the partnership agreement."

Marilyn Carlson Nelson has a vision for Carlson Companies that goes to the fifth or sixth generation of her family. A similar goal is held by Janice Bryant Howroyd of ACT 1. Both of these women are successful and accomplished entrepreneurs whose strategic vision is always top-of-mind. Partner relationships for these two are reviewed through the lens of ownership and ultimate control of the direction of the company. I once heard Hugh McColl, former CEO of Bank of America (by way of NationsBank), state that in his entire career, none of the banks he led were ever "acquired;" he was always the one doing the acquiring. It is important to know your own long term goals for yourself and your company as you review your partnership and alliance options.

To offer a personal example, my parents, Fred and Gert, bought a summer home in partnership with another couple,

Joe and Vivian, with whom they were quite close. They had vacationed together frequently, even rented cottages for a week or two at a time and got together in between for movie dates, card parties or just dinner and conversation. Sadly, Vivian developed cancer and passed away. After a while, Joe began to date and eventually remarried. Both during the dating stage and the subsequent marriage, the relationship between the two couples changed dramatically. Sharing a small cottage was not going to work for either partner. The new wife wanted more luxurious venues for her vacations and suggested using the property to generate rental income. A valid point of view, but not one shared by my mother. The partnership no longer worked. Fortunately, Fred and Joe were still close enough friends to have an "amicable divorce." My dad bought out Joe's share.

What if you or your partner's personal circumstances change? If Fred and Joe's partnership had involved a money-generating business instead of a summer cottage, I believe we all know that the end result would have involved attorneys. You must prepare for changes in circumstances at the very beginning, when you are "in love."

JUST-IN-TIME LEARNING: Remember Those Relationship Rules

Just as brides and grooms need to have a clear understanding of each other's financial goals, consensus on the desired number of children, and compatible religious values, so do prospective professional partners need to clearly state their own goals for the business now, and in the future as well, in order to understand their prospective partner's goals.

Harkening back to those 11 Keys to a Successful Marriage/Relationship in Chapter One, business partners need to (#3) allow for influence by their partner, (#5) know themselves reasonably well, (#6) respect their partner's dreams, and (#8) share goals and practice teamwork in the relationship. If there are (#9) good conflict resolution skills in the relationship, then (#10) the "romance" in the relationship will survive.

While no one wants to enter a marriage, or a partnership of any sort, thinking that it might end (at least I hope they do not!), you have to be realistic and careful. I might point to the prominence of prenuptial agreements as an example—the 50 percent divorce rate in the United States is an undeniable reality.

FAST FACTS

When partnerships work, the payoff can be big. A.T. Kearney research shows that companies that achieve partnering excellence can enjoy a 25 percent greater increase in share value than their industry peers. But there's a catch: The success rate of strategic relationships is abysmally low. Their research indicates that 50 percent of partnerships and up to 70 percent of supply chain alliances fail to achieve their objectives.
- From "The Partnering Paradox," by Anne Deering, Charles Davis and Bill Markham, Executive Agenda, Volume 6, Number 2, Copyright 2005, A.T. Kearney, Inc.

While you can and should hope for the best in personal and professional relationships (and a prenuptial agreement is certainly a very personal choice), in business I believe you must always prepare for the possibility of the very worst—or the very best! For instance, what if someone were to offer to purchase your company for a dollar amount that you find to be generous, but your partner does not want to sell because she enjoys running the company more than acquiring greater riches? It is a simply good, smart practice to enter into any professional relationship with a clear understanding of the consequences of its ending. In business, "happily ever after" may mean something different to different people.

For instance, Jodi Clausman and Kelly Hess of Global Legal, a Global Strategic Sourcing Company, make sure that all of their company's alliance partners understand their exit strategy before entering into the partnership. "Everybody should have an exit strategy," says Jodi. "We have had to explain that to all of our alliance partners....Our goal is to become the largest full-service litigation support company in the nation....We have to create as much value as possible in the company so that eventually we can do an IPO.

"Another mistake that I believe a lot of woman- and minority-owned businesses make is that they are too focused on what they want to accomplish and have not put a lot of thought into 'Then what?' They are too much into right here, right now, and not thinking about the long-term and how they are going to get out. Hopefully, all five of our alliance partners will end up multimillionaires in three to five years. That is our exit strategy." Not a bad goal!

Why Partnerships Fail

To begin any partnership with your eyes wide open, keep in mind these most common reasons for the failure of relationships. According to the American Academy of Matrimonial Lawyers, from which this list is drawn, not all marriages fail for the same reasons, nor is there usually just one reason for the breakdown of a particular marriage. However, the following reasons are most often cited by divorcing couples:

- Poor communication
- Financial problems
- Lack of commitment to the marriage/relationship
- A dramatic change in priorities
- Infidelity

I would argue that these same concepts are responsible for breaking up business partnerships as well. They also relate back to at least three of the five building blocks of partnership:

- Financial problems—BUILDING BLOCK: FINANCIAL RESOURCES
- Lack of commitment to the marriage/relationship—BUILDING BLOCK: TIMING
- A dramatic change in priorities—BUILDING BLOCK: STRATEGIC VISION

One might also argue that the building block support networks could help out with that infidelity problem!

In my opinion, the first questions that should go through your mind when you meet a potential partner are directly related to these hot button issues:

- Is this a good time for each of us to consider a partnership?
- Do we share financial values and open our books to each other?
- How well do we communicate with one another?
- Are we equally committed to making this partnership work?
- Do we each have the necessary human resources and personal support networks?
- Can we agree to our top priorities and plan to reassess them on a regular basis?
- Do I trust this person to be loyal to me and our partnership terms?
- Do we share goals and a vision of how our partnership will grow or end?

Once again, the building blocks are visible in this important partnership planning stage. Note that many of these issues will come up again in Chapter Six when we address partnership agreements and contracts. Beyond agreeing in theory about goals, shared duties and exit strategies, you will want to officially commit to these important building block issues in writing.

JUST-IN-TIME LEARNING: Consider a Mediator

Most people think of going to a mediator when relationships run into problems, but why not use this service at the beginning of a partnership? According to Ronnie Feit, an independent business consultant active in the women's business community, getting existing or proposed business principals to participate in professionally mediated discussions with each other is one good way to clarify problem areas and see what can be done to avoid or clear them up. (See further discussion of mediation in Chapter Eight.)

Dawn Martin, Esq., President of Martin Mediation Group, LLC in Washington, DC, shares this information:

"Our mediation company provides businesses with experienced mediators—women and men, many of whom are multilingual—with business, organizational development, legal and psychology backgrounds, as needed. These experts have a record of successfully helping existing and potential principals of partnerships, closely held corporations or joint ventures to recognize, anticipate, deal with or prevent the personal and business concerns that could cause trouble. In all these forms of doing business, it is often hidden issues that lead to problems. Mediation can surface these, prevent or end blaming, and help principals deal with such issues successfully."

Now that we have taken a glimpse at the way partnerships can end, we can feel a little wiser as we go back to discussing the beginning of a partnership: the dating or courtship phase.

The Ultimate Matchmaker Checklist

As with Chapter Two, the format of this chapter boils down to a series of questions that you need to ask about a potential partner. You can use this checklist repeatedly with various partners.

WORDS OF WISDOM:
The Most Important Definition of "Partnership"

"In any partnership, both parties should share the same definition of the word 'partnership.'"
- Jo Ann Brumit, Chairman and CEO, KARLEE, Garland, Texas

Business Basics

- Do you view your partner as your equal?
- Do you respect the products and/or services offered by the potential partner?
- Is it clear how this partnership will benefit both parties?
- Does the partner have a good reputation/strong brand?
- Can we fill each other's business gaps and reduce duplication?

What other partnership relationships does this business have? According to WBE Ranjini Poddar, President of Artech Information Systems in Morristown, New Jersey, "An important element for business owners looking at potential partners is to review that organization's prior successful partnerships within the same industry to evaluate their business practice history and success track record."

WORDS OF WISDOM

"Marriage is not just spiritual communion; it is also remembering to take out the trash."
- Dr. Joyce Brothers

Leadership Style and Values

- Do you and your potential partner share values?
- What are your potential partner's priorities? Ranjini Poddar points out the importance of sharing a vision in terms of technology and globalization: "Business owners," she says, "must evaluate a potential partner to decide if they share common business values and goals. For example, does the potential partner emphasize a global perspective and implement emerging technologies through their business as your business does, or has their focus been on managing existing accounts in the United States while utilizing older, existing technology? A common goal to grow together on the same foundation is key to avoiding a cracked base down the road."
- What are the skills and areas of expertise of the potential partner and how do those compare to your own?
- Can we fill each other's personal gaps and reduce duplication?
- How often does the partner want to communicate and in what format? Will you have weekly scheduled meetings, daily e-mails, or other ways of keeping in touch?

If the answers to these questions make you feel uneasy, you may want to consider an acquisition rather than a partnership. If you want to buy the capacity, reputation and/or product, but not the boss, you should make an offer for a buyout rather than negotiating a partnership.

Finding Your Complement

Jodi Clausman and Kelly Hess, mentioned above, are 50-50 partners in Global Strategic Sourcing and their relationship appears to be a match made in heaven: They bring different skills to the table—Kelly is "the organizer" and Jodi is "the visionary"—but their value system appears to be in perfect alignment. So much so, in fact, that they finish each other's sentences…and even wear the same clothes:

"Jodi and I make a dynamic team," says Kelly. "We end up making one person. In fact, we used to go into client meetings and realize we were dressed the same! Eventually we would shop together to deliberately buy different things!"

On a more serious note, Jodi and Kelly share a total commitment to customer service. "What our clients feel from both of us is honesty," Kelly says. "We care about them and their products and services. When we get a job in—whether providing a person or a service [Global Strategic Sourcing's Global Legal division currently serves many Fortune 500 clients that need legal support services]—it is as if we are sitting in our client's office with the services we provide.... We really care about them."

Roz Alford and Nancy Williams of ASAP Staffing are another example of complementary leadership styles working well in a partnership situation: "Nancy has the sales ability and I have the nurturing and people skills to balance the partnership and make it work," Roz says. "You have to know when to use one and when to use the other. We have always been able to sense which of us is making the best headway with a client. It is like a 'good cop, bad cop' situation. Not all clients like us equally. You cannot have two like personalities running a business. Your company needs to be a diverse melting pot. But we do have common goals, with a different approach on how to get there. And, when it gets into a critical situation with a client, we make a decision together and stand behind it."

Logistics

- How compatible are our corporate cultures? (That human resources building block comes into play here in a big way).
- How many points of contact will there be between our companies? Note that this is particularly important with David/Goliath partnerships.
- Will there be staff and real estate consolidations and how will that affect your current employees?

When I was running a women's business training center in the early '90s, one of the prevalent issues faced by growing businesses was what to do with loyal staff whose skills had not kept up with the growth of the business. Do you have employees whose own abilities will be challenged in the new corporate structure? Are there duplications in skills and titles? Have you considered what layoffs and buyouts will cost the new company and factored that into the partnership equation?

The Final Question

Does this person pass the "smell test" or "gut check"? Though not a scientific predictor of success by any means, I believe that we all have a bit of a sixth sense for personal relationships. If your intuition tells you that a potential partner "just feels wrong," I would take this as a sign that you may want to revisit some of the questions above, or triple-check his or her references for any sign that the partner may not be as ideal as he or she looks on paper. "If a partnership does not feel right, it will not work," says WBE Betsy Mordecai of MorSports & Events, Inc. "It is all about trust and relationship-building."

WORDS OF WISDOM: Success Factors

"In my opinion the most important success factors in any partnership are values, strategies and vision. If these are the underlying foundations of a partnership, any obstacles can usually be worked through. Add to those factors honesty, integrity, compromise, flexibility and keeping an open mind. All of these combined lead to a very trusting environment that will allow partnerships to thrive, even through crisis situations."
- Pat Birmingham, Associate Director, Vendor Management, Pfizer Global Sourcing

Much of a "gut check" relates to the sharing of deeply held values. On this topic, I will again share a personal story of my own. Many years ago I was in a serious dating relationship with a man who was always late. Everyone thought we would get married, and we had discussed that option on many occasions ourselves. As one who is compulsively punctual, I could not get past my potential significant other's constant late arrivals, delayed meals and excuses to our friends. I believed (and still believe to this day) that someone who is late does not value your time. And if someone does not value your time, how can he value you? If a partnership is a marriage and a marriage a partnership, can one enter into either if there is not total respect on both sides? I do not think so. I ended the relationship.

WORDS OF WISDOM: In Partnerships We Trust

Trust was the quality most commonly cited by interviewees for this book as the number one criterion for a solid, successful partnership. Here are the details, in their own words:

"If it is truly a two-way partnership, the commitment and relationship will be wonderful. If there is not trust on both sides, the partnership will probably not survive."

- Ellie Halter, CEO, Schnipke Engraving Co., Ottoville, Ohio

"Trust and honesty are, in my opinion, the most important success factors [in a partnership]. I don't like to 'play games.'"
- Pamela C. Shafer, President, New Orleans Copper, Inc., New Orleans, Louisiana

Putting Yourself "Out There"

It is a common refrain among single people of all ages: "Where are all the good men and women?" I hear this question from GMEs as well. A high-quality man, woman or partner is quite hard to find. Thinking through all of the qualities you want in any type of partner is a critical first step, but it will mean nothing unless you cast a wide net and start looking for people who have the qualities you are seeking. If you are considering an acquisition and not a partnership, many of the same questions need to be asked. What are you looking for in the company and, even if the current owner will not be in the picture, what kind of corporate culture, businesses processes and brand image will remain? When business owners and single friends alike consult with me about how to meet a partner, I recommend the same foolproof strategy: networking.

No matter how successful you are today, you must get out there in every way to make the connections that will lead you to profitable partnerships to take your business into the future. Networking to find a business partner or a candidate for an acquisition must be done strategically and frequently. By placing yourself in the right situations—online, at live events and through personal and professional contacts—you are bound to find suitable partners. Don't forget that while technology like "Live Meetings™" can save time and travel while providing information, a little "high touch" with face to face opportunities is also important. The good news is that your best potential partner, whether for a formal partnership or a strategic alliance, is likely out there looking to meet you as well.

In October of 2004, WBENC conducted a pilot for its new program, Zenith. Caroline Gundeck, First Vice President of Merrill Lynch and co-sponsor of the program, commented to me that the women were doing deals on the bus on their way to the opening event! One of those deals has now been formalized with a business opportunity involving Betty Manetta's Argent Technologies, a prime to a major contract and Lisa Hanlon's TelTech Communications as the tier two on the project.

JUST-IN-TIME LEARNING: Networking Secrets

In my opinion, you can never read too much on the topic of networking. Here is some wise guidance from an article by Olivia Fox Cabane, Executive Director of Spitfire Communications LLC, and author of several networking handbooks, including the recently published "Network Expansion Handbook."

Networking is more than just who you know; it is a process you can master and implement in any situation. Both MIT and the Harvard Business School recently recognized the need to teach their students how to "connect" by adding networking classes to their MBA programs. Well, if networking is so important, why doesn't everybody do it more often? One answer is the fear factor—namely, the fear of rejection. What if they don't want to talk to me? What if they ignore me? What if they—gasp—embarrass me?

True, your ego is at risk when you approach others. But isn't it true that the biggest regrets come from the risks you do not take? First, let me reassure you, if for no other reason than that it's bad for business, very few people are openly hostile or rude. And even if the person you approach seems disinterested, consider what may be going on in his or her mind—they may be somewhere else altogether. Have you ever experienced being so concentrated on a personal issue that when someone came up to talk to you, you brushed off that person without even realizing it?

Another problem is that many of us have been taught to avoid speaking with strangers, and to wait to be properly introduced before making contact. As adults, many of us are still waiting. What to do if you are not supposed to talk to strangers? Redefine the term! Say you are attending a graphic design conference and there is not a soul you know. You are not really with strangers when you have so much in common with the other attendees. It is more likely a question of how to connect rather than whether you can connect.

"But if I do a good job, is that not enough? Won't people come to me then?" Unfortunately we do not always get the introduction, the business referral or the return business just because we have done an outstanding job... so who does? Often, it is to the person who is on the top of the referrer's mind. In advertising, this is called "top-of-mind" awareness, and multinational companies spend billions of dollars trying to achieve it with you. With the proper networking techniques, you can achieve the same result—for free. Another issue that women, in particular, fight against, is the fear of appearing aggressive or pushy; we've always been taught that patience is a virtue. Unfortunately, waiting for people to find you and introduce themselves is useless. Since many people are shy or afraid of rejection they will not initiate contact; it is just as hard for them as it is for you. Do yourselves both a favor—go ahead and start!

So, you know networking is important, and you are ready to try. Where do you start? First, you need to know what your goals are: What do you want to accomplish? Now, what do you *really* want to accomplish? What would your life look like if you did? Be as specific as possible—you are giving your brain a road map to your ideal destination. What would your life look like if you got there?

Then, figure out what you need to do to reach these goals: Who are your targets? How many contacts do you need and in what area? Who are your competitors? What resources do you need, and where will you get them?

A good way to start is to create a diagram of your resources—your Network Diagram. Place yourself at the center of the page and map out the organizations and groups you belong to. Include institutions you have attended, companies where you have worked and the contacts you have in each. How big is your network? Actually, it is the size of all your contacts, plus all your friends' contacts, your peers' contacts, etc. Where are most of your contacts located by city, state or country? By industry? Look at each main hub: if the company or organization is an important client, what would happen if your main contact left?

Whenever you start a new project, your diagram can shed light on new opportunities and help you implement your approach. What' is more, once you see your network, you will realize which actions you need to take to optimize it by putting people in touch with each other. You will begin thinking about how some people's needs connect with other people's resources, just like a Rubik's Cube, until the pieces fall together.

Here are some recommended networking strategies for finding your partnership soul mate:

Start Looking Before You Need a Partner

This advice may sound like too little, too late, but it is also too true. You would not wait until the week before the prom to find a date, so analyze what key events are on the horizon for your industry and start planning as soon as possible. As with networking, marketing and sales prospecting, you need to think of partnering as a regular item on your to-do list rather than an "I will get to it when I need it" activity. Finding a good partner can take months, if not years, so you should always be on the lookout for potentially good alliance prospects. There also may be an opportunity for a "trial marriage" in terms of a strategic alliance on a specific business deal that might provide the critical insight into whether or not your building blocks add up to a new, improved structure.

Access Your Network

Put the word out to your clients, vendors, colleagues, fellow certified businesses and friends that you are seeking potential partners. WBE Mary Cantando, a "growth expert" and head of WomanBusinessOwner.com, offers the wise advice that looking out for other people's partnership needs will come in handy when you yourself are seeking a partner:

"Always be in the mode of looking out for others, doing things for others, helping others connect. I constantly have my mind open to identifying the needs of others, especially women business owners, and finding ways to support them. Of course the flip side of this habit is that whenever I need to ask a favor of anyone, I feel very comfortable doing so and they are always delighted to help me out."

Indeed, the more you give of your own network and resources, the more you can expect back when you are the one seeking a connection or referral. As Pat Birmingham of Pfizer says, "The strength of a solid reputation due to an existing partnership could be the catalyst for a supplier to be elevated in their field among that partner's network of business contacts."

Ask a Current Partner for a "Setup"

Remember that partners who know how well you do your job are an excellent source of referrals. As corporate supply chains continue to compress, smaller companies will need to form multiple partnerships to remain competitive, so take advantage of every opportunity. According to WBE Pamela C. Shafer, President/Owner, New Orleans Copper, Inc., "A partner expects the other to be truly concerned about their business relationship and is willing to help the advancement and growth of each other's business by referring them to others. The growth of one business will only help the other to grow."

FAST FACTS

When it comes to doing business with large corporations, the key success factor according to women business owners is having relationships with decision makers—fully 97 percent of respondents rated such relationships as either very or extremely important.
- WBEN/Center for Women's Business Research Access to Markets Study

Attend Networking Events

While networking events should already be part of your marketing strategy as a successful business owner, you should approach this activity a bit differently when you are looking for strategic alliance partners. If partnership is on your agenda as a key growth strategy, select which networking events to attend based on the likelihood that you will find partnership prospects there. When you are at an event, spread the word about what kind of partner(s) you are seeking—this is one place where your matchmaker profile comes in particularly handy. You do not need to give away too much information about why, when or how you are seeking to partner; just get the word out. As you will see in the Matchmaker Meetings section below, some networking events are entirely designed to help you find and connect with potential partners.

JUST-IN-TIME LEARNING:
You are Your Own Best Advertisement

Nely Galán was musing after the birth of her son that she would like her pre-baby body back. She allowed herself to daydream and think about what she would want that would be absolutely wonderful.

"I thought about five months at a spa where I would be pampered and fed healthy, delicious food. And then I thought, a boob job might not be bad either."

That daydream ultimately became "The Swan," Nely's successful ABC reality TV series that provides life-altering extreme makeovers that transform the proverbial "ugly duckling" into a beautiful swan. At the Office Depot Success Strategies for Women Conference in February, 2005, Nely received the Business Entrepreneur Visionary Award.

Throughout the conference Nely was front and center, telling everyone about her new program idea, "Ms. Mogul," and letting everyone know that she was looking for financial partners to launch the program. Nely's arsenal of networking tools included a winning personality, a sign she carried with her about Ms. Mogul that in bold type clearly outlined her needs, and an approachable demeanor that brought her in contact with potential funders as well as women entrepreneurs who could provide content and even participation in her next project.

As you can see, Nely made quite an impression on me and she will come to mind if I meet anyone in the field of television production.

Some organizations hosting events that may be sources for potential alliance partners include:

- Certification organizations like WBENC and the National Minority Supplier Development Council (NMSDC) and their local affiliates (see below for more information about maximizing your relationship with this invaluable resource)

- Local Chambers of Commerce
- Women's organizations such as the National Association of Women Business Owners (NAWBO) or Women in Technology International (WITI)
- Diversity Organizations such as the U.S. Pan Asian American Chamber of Commerce, U.S. Hispanic Chamber of Commerce or the African American Chamber of Commerce
- Government agencies, which host events such as the NASA/JPL High Tech Small Business Conference.

I mention the NASA conference specifically because of an e-mail I received from NASA Assistant Administrator Ralph Thomas recently, in which he shared this rave review from an event attendee:

"I'm looking forward to being part of JPL this year, as I came back with so many great contacts last year. The best part of last year was the funding we did as a result of the financing panel you put together. I met [an entrepreneur] who was looking for funding to help him perform on NASA contracts. Once we both returned to the DC area, we worked together to set up a line of credit large enough for him to not only perform on current contracts, but also to demonstrate to NASA that he could ramp up and perform on new contracts as well."

Why is this event—as well as others like it—so important for GMEs seeking business with particular government agencies and seeking other companies with which to partner? The conference, according to its organizers, serves as a one-stop event in that all of the NASA field centers are represented, as well as all of NASA's prime contractors. In addition, more than a hundred other major corporations, federal and state agencies, and universities exhibit as buyers.

FAST FACTS

Among WBE companies who are currently marketing to Fortune 1000 corporations, seven in ten (70 percent) say that they develop personal relationships with supplier diversity/purchasing professionals as part of their external marketing and sales efforts to large corporations. Other marketing and sales efforts include preparing marketing materials specifically for large corporate customers (62 percent) and having membership in local or national women's business organizations (59 percent).
- WBENC/Center for Women's Business Research Access to Markets Study

Like WBENC's annual national conference, JPL is filled with substantive workshops. Theirs deal primarily with how to obtain contracts and subcontracts from NASA and it provides numerous networking opportunities for small businesses that are serious about facilitating partnerships with NASA, its prime contractors, and/or others. Be on the lookout for other such events, through various event calendars. Here is a list of a few I recommend:

- Women's Business Development Center in Chicago, every September (*www.wbdc.org*)
- Women's Business Enterprise Alliance in Houston (*www.wbea-texas.org*)
- Women's Business Council Southwest, each May (*www.wbcsouthwest.org*)
- Michigan Women's Business Council, every October (734-677-1400)
- Office Depot Success Strategies for Businesswomen Conference, every February/March
- U.S. Hispanic Chamber of Commerce, every fall (September/October)
- National Minority Supplier Development Council, every October

PROFITABLE PARTNERSHIP:
Burgoon Company and Grainger Industrial Supplies

Galveston, Texas-based Burgoon Company is a laboratory, medical, and safety equipment and supply company, founded and run by Nita Burgoon. According to Nita, at the WBENC National Conference a few years ago, Jan Wynn, General Manager for Burgoon Company, connected with then-new WBENC corporate member Grainger Industrial Supplies, as a potential supply ally.

Nita says, "From that expo, Burgoon Company has become the largest distributor for Grainger nationwide, and a strategic supply ally on the State of Texas TXMAS contract, as well as other government business, with sales in excess of $5,000,000 annually.

"By working together, Burgoon and Grainger have partnered for success, which all started at WBENC!"

JUST-IN-TIME LEARNING: Never Stop Networking

My husband is fond of saying that I start a receiving line every time I enter a room. The truth is, I love people and am energized in crowds. It would be a rare event for me to walk away from a networking opportunity without a new lead or a personal introduction to someone I have wanted to meet. Networking is second nature, but even a natural networker like me has benefited by speeches and books by networking gurus. That's why conferences such as WBENC's own Women in Business conference are such a win-win for me and for all participants. Business fairs, keynotes and receptions provide networking opportunities and workshops help to hone our skills. One such session at a conference I attended a decade ago advised that prior to attending a formal networking event one should keep four things in mind:

- Have a specific, well-articulated and practiced goal that you want to accomplish in the limited time slot of the networking opportunity. For example, you want to get a reference to find a specific type of supplier or the contact information for a key corporate contact.

- Know what you have to offer to others in the room. People will be more willing to share information with you if you make it clear that you have valuable information as well.
- Get at least one business card of someone with whom you will follow up after the event.
- To maximize the effectiveness of networking, keep records: a diary, notes in an electronic format or even just on the back of a business card. I can attest from personal experience that our memories are not all we think and hope they are.

Life offers networking opportunities nearly every day. Earlier in my career, I was the director of a Federal agency, The Institute of Museum Services (IMS). (For the only time in my career, I got to hand out money without having to go out and raise it first.) The Agency provided funding to museums, zoos, historical societies, botanical gardens and such. I got that prestigious and interesting position from networking, pursuing contacts, and making the business case for hiring me! A couple of years into my term, at one of Washington's endless receptions, I ran into the White House Presidential Personnel Associate Director, Maryann Urban, whose recommendation to the President had led to my appointment at IMS. "What's new?" I asked, and was surprised to find out that Maryann was leaving her job and moving to Pennsylvania to pursue a personal partnership. "Oh no," I thought out loud, "if you leave, who will be my contact?" Maryann's next utterance was to ask me if I was interested in being considered for her job. Two weeks later I was sitting in my office in The White House.

For much more on the topic of networking see Chapter Four of Breaking Through: Creating Opportunities for America's Women and Minority Owned Businesses.

Take Full Advantage of Your Certification Organization

Among the services of your certification organization and its local affiliates is to help the business growth of its members, including helping to introduce potential partners to one another. Do not miss out on this huge resource that exists to assist you! I am consistently surprised and dismayed to learn how few certified businesses take advantage of this amazing opportunity. Kate Chrisman, Executive Director of the Women's Business Council Gulf Coast, WBENC's New Orleans-based partner organization, explains:

"For every active member that we have, we have 20 inactive WBEs. These inactive WBEs never come to any of our networking functions, never use the resources on our web site or the national WBENC web site and never take advantage of any of the free press and marketing opportunities that our council provides its members. This is very frustrating to the staff, as well as the corporate partners, whose annual dues provide these opportunities that go unused. The main purpose of all of our activities is to 'match' our WBEs with our corporate partners. However, the fringe benefit of these functions is meeting and networking with other certified WBEs. These are invaluable opportunities to meet potential partners with whom to align yourself and your company.

"Furthermore, the WBEs that are constantly in my peripheral vision—attending our events, coming to our committee meetings, sending me e-mail updates about their companies, etc.—are the ones I use as examples when I am serving as a panelist or giving a speech about the Women's Business Council Gulf Coast. Want me to promote your company? Get in front of my face! Make yourself known to me. I cannot promote you if I do not know you or your story."

If I were a betting person, I would add that I bet those uninvolved WBEs are the same ones that complain that "certification never did anything for me." I emphasize over and over to the

GMEs I meet that attending a conference/business fair is not time away from your business; rather, it is bringing your business to a new, more fertile location.

About a week after WBENC's Women in Business 2004 conference I received a call from one of our newer WBEs, Julia Klein, CEO of C.H. Briggs. WBENC Vice President Linda Denny and I had heard Julia speak at a conference in May, and when we discovered she was newly certified we encouraged her to exhibit at our business fair. (As you can see, we at WBENC benefit from networking as well as you.) Julia's call was to invite Linda and me to lunch, where she thanked us profusely for encouraging her to attend Women in Business 2004: Sharing the Vision Julia explained that she brought three other people from her company so that two of them could "walk the floor" to meet targeted corporate representatives, and two stay back in the booth to provide information on their products. Julia reported that the strategy worked well and that she was able to connect with companies on her target list. She also discovered a previously unconsidered market for her company's products.

Even though she personally will not be able to attend the next conference, her company will exhibit and send a full complement of staff to take advantage of the many opportunities provided. "There is one thing I don't understand," Julia stated, "Why doesn't every certified WBE take advantage of this incredible opportunity?" I do not understand it either. When I was a manufacturer's representative, I travelled a six-state territory to find my customers. At the Women in Business congefence, the corporate customers for our WBEs are all in one room and their attention is directed solely at you.

After reading *Breaking Through,* which Julia received at the conference thanks to a sponsorship from KPMG to provide the book to all attendees, she then purchased 10 more copies to distribute to her entire sales team.

Ask Corporate Customers

Whether you are already a supplier to a major corporation or you are looking to partner to win your first contract, consider seeking advice and connections from corpote supplier diversity professionals. Helping GMEs access each other is part of their job description. Just ask Keith Hines, "Most corporations are willing to offer advice on an alliance," he says. "In my line of work, we are on the phone with entrepreneurs every business day of the year. We are actively pointing them in the right direction and providing advice."

Kathy Greco of Manpower Professional agrees. "Do not be afraid to ask the advantage of partnering with a bigger company and find out the details of working together," she says, specifically referring to GMEs looking for David/Goliath-style alliances. "We are happy to share information on things like how and where to obtain insurance to make sure smaller companies are qualified to work with us."

What could be more helpful than potential large-scale customers telling you exactly what they recommend? Do not hesitate to access this network of experienced and highly connected people.

PROFITABLE PARTNERSHIP:
ASAP Staffing and SBC Communications

At the WBENC Salute to Women's Businesses in 2003, Nancy Williams and Roz Alford of ASAP Staffing met Joan Kerr, Executive Director of Supplier Diversity Programs at SBC Communications. Here is the story of how that meeting—and smart strategic vision and follow-through—led to a profitable partnership:

Nancy says, "I called Joan about a month after [the Salute] and sent information on the company. We had already decided to attend WBENC's Women in Business conference in New York that June. Through Joan, we were invited to have refreshments with Maureen Merkle, who had just been made SBC's President of Procurement. We met with them for two hours. Throughout the meeting there were discussions on the course of action necessary to work with SBC. One involved the possibility of working with SBC's current prime suppliers, such as Accenture. We were already working with Accenture on another account as second tier, something we had done before and with which we were very comfortable.

"It took about four months of meetings in San Ramon, California, and we were given our first opportunity with SBC in January 2004. Within a period of eleven months we were able to place fourteen consultants with revenue generation of $1 million. The reason this is so key is that it proved to SBC that, though we are located in Atlanta, we could support their needs in Chicago, San Ramon and St. Louis. Through that support and continued relationship building, we were able to participate in an RFI for their entire company and just submitted another RFP."

Nancy's partner Roz adds, "On another note, at the conference in New Orleans in June, 2004, ASAP bid and won a Power Lunch with Maureen Merkle. It solidified the commitment of SBC even more. In that meeting, she brought one of her IT sourcing leaders, Andrew Jones, and we had the opportunity to talk about their current state of business."

Nancy explains, "I had already done the research through newspapers and web sites, so I was pretty up on their direction. Going back to thinking outside the box, we were able to propose new solutions to them that would meet their objectives at reduced cost. Because Maureen was impressed with our approach, we were also able to meet with her Vice President of sourcing.

"Because of WBENC, we were able to make a connection that we might never have gotten, no matter how good we are at marketing. Maureen does not meet with many companies at this level—Presidents seldom do. WBENC made it happen."

According to Roz, "You have to know how to work it. Most people would not have done the research and due diligence to make it happen. Most would not have spent the money to bid on the Power Lunch. You have to understand the opportunity and the costs involved. Once you get certified, you have to work even harder than before you were certified. The contacts are there, but all the other certified companies are approaching them as well. You have to differentiate yourself."

Formal Matchmaker Meetings

WBENC and other certification organizations even provide opportunities for GMEs to access the knowledge and contact files of supplier diversity professionals. WBENC's MatchMaker Meeting Series, for example, connects WBENC-certified WBEs with corporate purchasing officials for private face-to-face meetings to discuss potential opportunities.

WBENC's listserv, *WBENC-Discuss@wbenc.org,* notifies all certified WBEs of upcoming MatchMaker meetings. WBEs apply to attend these meetings by completing a WBE Profile Sheet and application attached to the notification e-mail for each specific MatchMaker meeting in which they wish to participate. These forms are then used by the MatchMaker Corporation's purchasing personnel, along with a supplier's WBENCLink profile, in the selection process. (A reminder to make sure your WBENC profile—and any online profile—is always current!) Attendees are then selected for this mega-opportunity to meet with corporations that have pre-selected you.

When you attend a MatchMaker meeting, use the opportunity to discuss strategic alliance issues with the purchasing executive you meet. You may find that they can facilitate an introduction to another supplier that will increase your chances of winning a contract with their corporation, or you may find that the corporation itself is a potential alliance partner.

Online Opportunities

The Internet abounds with opportunities to find potential partners. Here is some guidance to find your perfect match on the World Wide Web:

For WBENC members and WBEs:

WEBuy@wbenc.org is another reason for WBENC-certified WBEs to keep profiles up to date in WBENCLink. Corporate members, government agencies, WBENC itself and WBEs post opportunities in the form of RFPs, RFQs and Sources Sought. If you want someone in your firm in addition to or other than yourself to receive this valuable tool, e-mail *B2B@wbenc.org* and write "subscribe" in the subject line. In addition to WEBuy, WBENC provides information on upcoming events of interest, including procurement fairs sponsored by our partner organizations, corporate members and government agencies in our monthly e-newsletter, *"President's Report."*

For everyone:

One of the frequent complaints I receive is the time and effort it takes to register on numerous corporate databases after going through the certification process of either WBENC or the NMSDC. My advice is: "Stop complaining. Get over it and just do it. This is an opportunity." I do not understand why anyone would consider it a burden to register for an opportunity. Corporations use WBENC, NMSDC, and their own databases to search for suppliers and to notify you of upcoming opportunities, both in terms of specific procurement opportunities and special procurement and diversity events sponsored by the corporation.

For businesses interested in supplying to the federal government:

If you are seeking a teaming arrangement to supply to the federal government, the SBA's Office of Government Contracting's Contract Assistance for Women Business Owners (CAWBO) unit recommends accessing the Federal Business Opportunities (FedBizOpps) web site. It is the government's single point of entry for federal government procurement opportunities over $25,000. Small businesses seeking federal procurements can search, monitor and retrieve opportunities solicited by the entire federal government. The web address for FedBizOpps is *www.fedbizopps.gov*.

The Small Business Administration's (SBA) SUB-Net is another site where small businesses can search for procurement opportunities, including teaming arrangements. Prime contractors post solicitations on the SUB-Net site. Solicitations are reviewed by SBA personnel for accuracy in text content. Accurate solicitations are activated by SBA personnel and the prime contractor is given a password to post additional solicitations. The web address for SUB-Net is *http://web.sba.gov/subnet*. Small businesses are also potential teaming partners. The Central Contractor Registration (*www.ccr.gov*), which now incorporates the SBA's PRO-Net function, is an excellent resource to use to search for teaming partners.

PROFITABLE PARTNERSHIP: Manpower and S.J. Bailey

Kathy Greco, Director of the Supplier Diversity Program at Manpower Professional, shares this alliance story:

After spending 10 years working in the staffing business in Cincinnati, Stephen Bailey was bit by the entrepreneurial bug. He had a vision of a staffing company that connected those most in need of jobs with employment opportunities. He wanted to help the economically disadvantaged find steady work. In October, 1999, he opened S.J. Bailey Inc. with a mission to provide tempto-perm job opportunities in the Cincinnati area.

"I want people to see that employment is the gateway to a better lifestyle," says Bailey. "Employment gives people the courage to set goals and the tools to achieve them."

Bailey built a strong foundation and his business proved successful. Within three years, he was placing 250-500 people per week. S.J. Bailey employees averaged 30 to 40 days on the company's payroll before transitioning to permanent jobs with customers. But he did not intend to stop in Cincinnati; he wanted a national footprint for S.J. Bailey.

Bailey focused on mining new opportunities and networking within the business community in order to find the resources that would help him take S.J. Bailey to the next level. In 2001, he became acquainted with Kimmel Arn, area manager for Manpower in Cincinnati. Arn was seeking a diversity supplier for a major, national account. After one relationship did not work out, he started contacting other suppliers in the area, including Bailey.

"Steve and I clicked right away," reports Arn. "We agree that service and quality are highly important to our business. More importantly, we believe that honesty is integral to a mutually beneficial partnership."

Their shared philosophies grew into a successful partnership, and together they have been providing temporary staff to the customer since February 2002.

As their relationship continued, Bailey discussed his goal of taking S.J. Bailey to a national level with Arn. Based on the success of their partnership and Bailey's thriving business, Arn recommended Bailey as a candidate for Manpower's Diversity Supplier Mentoring Partnership Program. The program offers mentoring, partnership and internship programs to diversity suppliers who enhance Manpower's customer offerings. Bailey recognized that this was the opportunity he had been seeking, and he began the on-boarding process with Manpower's Vendor

Operations division at its corporate headquarters in Milwaukee.

"I knew this was the right program for me," says Bailey. "It embraced honesty, sincerity and integrity, qualities that were lacking in other programs I investigated."

Bailey submitted extensive background information about his business, such as delivery capability, financial strength and goals. Upon analysis, Vendor Operations determined that Bailey was the kind of partner Manpower was seeking for the program.

"Steve has great processes and goals in place, a willingness to learn, and the desire and capability to expand his operations," says Kathy Greco. "He is willing to be part of a true partnership where we open doors for each other."

And doors have been opening. Manpower has presented Bailey with opportunities to work with them on major, national accounts in Phoenix and other areas in Ohio. Those contracts allowed Bailey to open a second office in Scottsdale, Arizona, where he is off to a strong start.

Manpower has benefited too. Bailey is involved with minority business councils in Ohio, Arizona, Illinois and Indiana, and has brought Manpower into the fold with those groups. He has also recommended sponsorship opportunities that assist Manpower in raising awareness of their supplier diversity programs.

"In the relatively short time we have worked together, it has become obvious that together we can accomplish so much more than we can individually," says Bailey. "We have complementary strengths that take us to new heights."

Are you Ready to Write Your Own Profitable Partnership Story?

As you can see from this wide array of partnership situations, developing a partnership—even when the partners are loving family members—takes an enormous amount of planning, patience and negotiation. The next chapter will help you navigate the delicate, and occasionally downbeat, dance of the partnership.

Chapter Five

Who is on Top? Negotiating the Personal Side of Partnership

By this point you have identified the business or businesses you perceive to be your best prospective partners. Now we move from the "dating phase" into the longer-term courtship. Yes, I am talking about the "c" word: commitment. Now it is time to talk turkey: can this really work? No matter how much you love someone or they fit your ideal of a mate "on paper," you cannot have a relationship unless that person loves and respects you back and the two of you can live together in harmony (well, most of the time at least).

No matter how much you believe the maxim "business is business," you cannot deny that even the most formal business arrangement involves relationships between living, breathing human beings. The personalities, mood swings, emotions, goals and impulses of those human beings are as varied as the unique products and services their companies produce. This chapter helps you negotiate the delicate balance of power between partnering businesses. Ego and personality play a huge role in the partnership dynamic, so be prepared for some serious introspection. As those of us who are married or in long-term relationships know very well, no matter how much you love someone, a relationship is all about compromise.

WORDS OF WISDOM

"A good partner delivers, doesn't complain and rolls with the punches."
- Marsha Firestone, Ph.D.
President, Women Presidents' Organization and Women Presidents' Educational Organization

Making the Approach

Your first order of business before approaching any entity you identify for a partnership is to do your homework. Virtually every corporate supplier diversity professional I have ever met has emphasized the importance of research for GME suppliers. Nothing is more irritating than a supplier who attempts to sell a product or service that the corporation does not even buy. The same holds true for partnerships. Before you approach anyone, even for a conversation, you must research their business top to bottom.

WBE Janice Pellar, President of EMCO Technologies in Baton Rouge, Louisiana, explains what she recommends to companies that approach her for an alliance:

1. Do your homework about our company and know our focus areas and markets.
2. Prepare a value proposition of those things you as a partner bring to the relationship.
3. Have a broad general statement of your initial plans, ready to present.

In the spirit of doing *my* homework, I asked WBEs, corporate supplier diversity professionals and other business leaders how *they* like to be approached. You will see many themes throughout their answers—do your homework, share values—but you will also note significant differences. This should be a sign that you can never, ever assume you know what a company is looking for in a potential partnership: you must always perform significant research and directly ask what a potential partner is seeking.

Here are some answers to the key question, "What do you look for in a potential partner?"

- "I am in an unusual business: the speaking profession. I look for partnerships that allow me to dovetail someone else's skill set and product offerings. For example, someone who is a keynoter might want me to open a session for her or we might have complementary skill sets to meet a client's consulting needs. As far as approaching me with a potential relationship, my highest priorities are integrity, authenticity and a quality outcome for the client. If someone already has a client who needs my services, they can approach me with an idea for combining, or they might bring their services to me to suggest how they align with my work." - Julia Hubbel, President, The Hubbel Group, Lakewood, Colorado

- "A good partner must be committed to developing relationships that will enhance intelligent and innovative workforce solutions. They must fit Manpower's corporate culture and values with a commitment to quality service. They must promote integrity and professionalism....We want companies to show that they have a culture of quality, honesty, enthusiasm and passion. And I like a company that says, 'We want to be become your partner!'" - Kathy Greco, Director of Supplier Diversity, Manpower Professional

- "The best way to approach KARLEE, Inc. for a partnership is to seek the value propositions that meet our needs or propose a new opportunity that brings value to the table. Similarly, we have found success in approaching other companies for partnership by seeking value propositions that meet that company's needs and clearly presenting our proposition supported with facts." - Jo Ann Brumit, Chairman and CEO, KARLEE, Inc., Garland, TX

- "A good partner looks for opportunities to offer innovative concepts to help grow the business, increase revenue or decrease costs, and promote positive brand awareness." - Lynn Boccio, Vice President, Cendant Corporation

The First Date: Starting the Partnership Conversation

Dating is relatively easy compared to the courtship phase of a business partnership. In romantic situations, one party asks the other party for a date. When I was a young woman, it was assumed that the man made the first approach, but I asked my husband out on our first date 18 years ago. Typically, the two meet in a public establishment, such as a coffee shop, a bar or a restaurant. In business relationships, the courtship is a bit more complicated. Do you meet in your office or the potential partner's? Do you speak on the phone first or send information by e-mail? Is a relationship best forged over a meal? Much of this is personal choice, but it is important to think about these issues. The way a partnership begins sets the tone for the days, months and possibly years to come.

Nancy Williams, partner with Roz Alford in ASAP Staffing, explains that it is a process, more than a single event. "We knew we could work in business together, so the issue for us to clarify was management philosophies. We had to assure ourselves that our overall goals were in sync. We went away together for weekends to see if we could get along. We did a lot of dinners and luncheons, got to know each other personally and asked one another pretty tough questions: What would you do in this situation, in that situation, etc. We had a lot to gain, but we also had a lot to lose. We found that we shared common interests and visions. Business partnership really is like a marriage: If you are not ultimately friends, it will be tough to ride through rough times."

Here are some additional tips for your first few partnership discussions:

- **Do not overpromise.** As Pamela C. Shafer, President/Owner, New Orleans Copper, Inc., New Orleans, Louisiana, says, "Business owners need to be realistic in their capabilities. Offering a service or product when you really cannot deliver it, either in a timely manner or of good quality, will catch up with you and ruin any reputation you have already developed. It can kill future relationships."
- **Be yourself.** "Once you develop a one-on-one relationship—meeting in person—anything is possible," says Bruce Perkins, Vice President and Manager of Supplier Diversity at Merrill Lynch. "Look them in the eye and tell them the truth. Be up front and tell them who you are—it works. Once you establish those relationships, it will be easier for you to be successful."
- **Do not look for perfection; look for cooperation.** As Marsha Firestone, President of the Women Presidents' Educational Organization, WBENC's New York and Washington, DC affiliate, wisely points out, "The best partner is not always the smartest or most creative. It is often the person who has a high level of flexibility in their behavior—cooperation. To have a good marriage,

alliance, tennis partner or friend, you have to have give and take. Sometimes, one or the other will be on top and you have to be willing to accept the rise and the fall."

The Other "C" Word: Communication

Just as we addressed the rules for a successful marriage or relationship in Chapter One, virtually every successful alliance we interviewed for this book spoke in depth about the supreme importance of constant, open communication between partners. While commitment—the famous "c" word in personal relationships—is incredibly important, it can lose its luster when day-to-day communication is not taking place.

Ralph G. Moore, President of Ralph G. Moore & Associates (RGMA) and an expert in woman- and minority-owned business development, emphasizes the importance of communication when he counsels entrepreneurs entering into alliances. "It all comes down to communication," he says. "Even before forming an alliance, most entrepreneurs are working 60 to 80 hours a week and in an alliance they have even more time committed. Everyone is so busy—it is possible that if you are feeling uncomfortable about something, your partner may not even be aware of it. We are all focused on what we need to get done. If the other person is assuming things are okay, you owe it to your partner to raise the issue."

JUST-IN-TIME LEARNING: Communicating During a Merger, Acquisition or Partnership Process

Some communications are more challenging than others. Joyce Bosc, WBE and President and CEO of Boscobel Marketing Communications in Silver Spring, Maryland (a former AWED client of mine!), shares her tips on communicating during a merger or acquisition—one of the more sensitive business experiences. These tips are very wise counsel for communicating during any alliance relationship, and will be expanded upon

throughout this chapter:
Mergers and acquisitions (M&A) between organizations have increased for a variety of reasons. Primarily, these are done to either help one organization reduce debt and/or to increase another organization's services. If transitioned strategically, this technique can benefit both parties, but statistics show that 65 percent of all mergers and acquisitions fail to meet expected productivity levels or profit margins.

Here are seven tips that will help M&A communications:
1. Communicate the reasons why the transition is being considered and how it will benefit the organization and all the stakeholders at the beginning of the process.
2. Consider the concerns of all your stakeholders such as your customers, suppliers, press, subcontractors, vendors and, most important, your employees.
3. Keep all your stakeholders updated and involved throughout the process.
4. Establish a consistent brand image for the new entity. Keep values and quality consistent throughout the M&A process.
5. Use multiple channels to reach stakeholders (via web site, newsletter, e-blast, news releases, etc.). Disperse information through the Internet, e-mail, mail and fax to reach all audiences.
6. Create web pages for customers and employees with updated information and FAQs.
7. Communicate frequently, face-to-face, with stakeholders at media tours, press conferences, purpose-built roadshow events and trade shows.

Do Your Due...Diligence

WORDS OF WISDOM

"Do your homework, research the company, seek references, see all of their materials and trust your instincts!"
- WBE Betsy Mordecai, President, MorSports & Events, Inc.

Due diligence is one of the most important phases of forming an alliance. Doing the hard work now will increase your chances for success in the future. Do not cut corners! Consider this wise advice from the *Harvard Business Review:**

[S]uccessful acquirers view due diligence as much more than an exercise in verifying data. While they go through the numbers deeply and thoroughly, they also put the broader, strategic rationale for their acquisitions under the microscope. They look at the business case in its entirety, probing for strengths and weaknesses and searching for unreliable assumptions and other flaws in the logic. They take a highly disciplined and objective approach to the process, and their senior executives pay close heed to the results of the investigations and analyses—to the extent that they are prepared to walk away from a deal, even in the very late stages of negotiations. For these companies, due diligence acts as a counterweight to the excitement that builds when managers begin to pursue a target.

Going Steady and Trial Marriage

Find the right partner but feel afraid of commitment? Sometimes you can test out a potential partnership, or prove your own value, by collaborating on a smaller project. Furthermore, if you are considering a partnership with an existing vendor or customer, you can begin to make your case for joining forces by impressing them in your current relationship.

---

* "When to Walk Away from a Deal," by Geoffrey Cullinan, Jean-Marc Le Roux, and Rolf-Magnus Weddigen, Harvard Business Review, Vol. 82, No. 4, April 2004.

As WBE Charline Guidry, Chairman and CEO of Diamond Oil Field Supply in Belle Chasse, Louisiana, says, "If approaching a customer, we always start by serving as a supplier to build a successful track record. If approaching a vendor, we always start by being a good customer, including timely payment of invoices."

Meet the Parents

Another way to vet a potential partner before jumping into bed together (figuratively, of course!) is to ask a trusted third party for an opinion about the match. Do your research and it is likely you can find some mutual client, former colleague, certification organization, professional association or other person who is familiar with both of your businesses and can offer an objective opinion. Alternatively, GME business development expert Ralph Moore recommends involving an unbiased third party before entering into a partnership. "Any time you can get an independent third-party opinion on your compatibility, you will benefit in the long run. Independent analysis is a positive thing."

He even takes this advice a step further, recommending that potential partners, "Find a devil's advocate: find the most negative person you know when you think you have it all together, and find out what they think is wrong. If you can survive that conversation and you still want to partner, then you really have something!"

When my husband and I were dating and it was starting to look serious, I asked one of my close women friends whether she liked Dick. She responded, "Not only do I like him, but I also like you better since you started dating him." That is the ideal you should be looking for in your partnership; an alliance where the whole is greater than the sum of the parts.

Meet the Family

Before you commit to a strategic alliance of any length or intensity level, a partnership or an acquisition, be sure to familiarize yourself with the culture, and especially the employees, of your potential partner company. As divorced parents know, you need at least the basic approval from your children before entering into a marriage that will extend the family to include a whole set of new people. Every situation cannot end up as harmoniously as The Brady Bunch.

JUST-IN-TIME LEARNING:

Is a monogamous relationship even necessary?

Pat Henriquez, former CEO of Management Alternatives, successfully balanced relationships with several federal government prime contractors, frequently teaming with six or seven different companies on bids for the same piece of government work. Pat was able to manage these relationships because they valued her as a small, woman-owned business that met their federal goals, but who also delivered as part of the team. Her reputation for competency was enhanced by a reputation for confidentiality and together they earned her the respect of the primes—and a place at the table as their team member.

Can Opposites Really Attract?

I have spent a lot of time so far talking about finding the right match, the perfect partner, or your business soul mate; but there are many examples of highly successful partnerships and alliances that are far from perfect. In fact, they are decidedly imperfect, and sometimes that is precisely what makes them profitable. Could you form a partnership with your opposite?

My own family history offers insight into opposites attracting and thriving in business. You will probably not be surprised to learn that I grew up in an entrepreneurial family. Both of my grandfathers were entrepreneurs, as was my father. Dad was in the insurance business and owned a brokerage firm with his brother Mitchell. They were polar opposites. Dad was the extrovert—the outside guy, the rainmaker. (I think I must have inherited a few of his genes.) My uncle was an introvert, the inside manager of process and staff. It worked well. My father was able to spend a lot of time out and about, meeting potential new clients and keeping existing customers happy. Breakfast at the neighborhood delicatessen became a networking event. He could do this safe in the knowledge that if someone called the office and needed something, Mitchell would be there to provide information or advice over the telephone.

Another "opposites attracting" story takes us into the political realm. Terry Neese and Barbara Kasoff, co-founders of Women Impacting Public Policy, represent the Republican and Democrat arms of their bi-partisan organization. How do they make it work? "Believe us, we are opposites," says Terry. "We argue, we discuss, we get angry and we laugh. But our great working relationship and friendship is the most important factor in our success. What keeps us on track is knowing what a difference we are making for our members—and the WIPP members are the lifeline of WIPP. Our positive 'team' mentality is what keeps us going." This is yet another example of win-win-win partnering: Terry wins, Barbara wins and their "customers"—over 505,000 WIPP members—win.

Barbara agrees that a shared vision is essential for partners, especially when they are opposites in personality or politics. "First, you have to agree on your ultimate goal. From a policy standpoint, ours was to engage women in the political process and to bring them together as a unified voice so that we would make a difference in our nation's capital and so that they would see a direct benefit to their business growth. From a personal standpoint, we are friends first; we may disagree on issues, but we respect each other and each other's values and opinions.

After that, the rest is easy."

Now that we have explored partnerships ranging from David and Goliath, to Ozzie and Harriet, to Donkeys and Elephants, it is time to make things official: The walk down the aisle! Chapter Six will cover the legal, financial, technological and certification-related aspects of various partnership types.

Dum, da, dum, dum...

PROFITABLE PARTNERSHIP:
Pinnacle Technical Resources and Merrill Lynch

This profitable partnership story demonstrates the many ways a GME can partner with a large corporation, on both a local and national level, and how both sides reap the benefits. The story comes from Helen A. Wathen, Wealth Management Advisor and Vice President at Merrill Lynch in Dallas, Texas.

"I met Nina Vaca, Founder and CEO of Pinnacle Technical Resources, at the WBC-Southwest's annual Round-Up trade show event in 2003. This was the second official event of Merrill Lynch's Women's Business Development initiative in Dallas, the goal of which is to seek out and help established women business owners succeed.

"Nina and I connected immediately, and it was apparent that she understood the true concept of partnership. What is more, it was immediately evident that her business savvy, integrity, focus, and charisma created a unique and highly marketable package; and I knew Nina would be a perfect partner for Merrill Lynch's women's initiative.

"Over the past two years, our relationship has truly blossomed into a partnership as Nina and I have become involved in various women's business initiatives together. With Nina's guidance, Merrill Lynch joined the Greater Dallas Hispanic Chamber of Commerce and was able to gain access to numerous affluent and influential Hispanic women in Dallas. In both 2003 and 2004, we nominated Pinnacle for the Inner City 100 award sponsored by Merrill Lynch. As we go to print, Pinnacle has made the final cut for the 2004 award and has a great shot at being one of the final winners. Merrill Lynch also sponsored Nina's membership in the Women President's Organization (WPO). Lastly, we helped Pinnacle connect with Bruce Perkins and the Merrill Lynch Supplier Diversity group as well as our information technology purchasing department.

"In June of last year, our business relationship grew even further, when, during a lunch conversation, I mentioned Merrill Lynch's competitive banking platform. Several weeks later, Pinnacle's CFO contacted us with an urgent need related to funding the firm's rapidly growing cash flow needs. Within 24 hours, we were able to commit to a level of funding (via Merrill Lynch Business Financial Services) that was four times the size of Pinnacle's existing loan. In addition, we provided an overall interest rate and loan structure that was more cost effective and more strategically aligned with Pinnacle's business needs. Today, Pinnacle views Merrill Lynch as its exclusive banking partner as a result of our ability to provide a broad array of business and personal financial services combined with our ability to deliver the full resources of the bank quickly and effectively.

"Over the two-year period from mid-2002 to mid-2004, Pinnacle grew its revenue base by an astounding thirteen times, resulting in numerous awards for both Nina and the company. At a national level, Nina was twice honored as the Hispanic Business Woman of the Year (2003 & 2004) by the United States Hispanic Chamber of Commerce. Subsequently, Nina was also honored as the 2004 Hispanic Entrepreneur of the Year by Hispanic Business Magazine (Infobusiness category), as a 2004 Distinguished Woman by Northwood University, and as a German Marshall Fund Fellow representing the U.S. abroad. In 2004, at its annual Salute to Women's Business Enterprise, WBENC recognized Nina nationally as one of its Women Business Stars.

"During that time, Pinnacle received an equal number of honors as a corporation. In 2004, it was selected 26th in the Dallas 100TM list of fastest growing companies, it was recognized nationally as Supplier of the Year (West Region) by the National Minority Supplier Development Council, and it was nominated by Ernst & Young for their prestigious Entrepreneur of the Year award. In the year prior, Pinnacle had swept three major local awards by being selected as the top woman-owned, top minority-owned, and top Hispanic-owned business in the Dallas Metroplex by WBENC, NMSDC and USHCC, respectively, a feat never before accomplished in the history of those three awards. Just last week, Pinnacle was again selected as the Woman-Owned Business of the Year for the second time in three years.

"Currently, Nina serves as Chair of the Greater Dallas Hispanic Chamber of Commerce, and as a Board Member and Executive Committee Member of the Women's Business Council - Southwest. She recently asked me to co-chair the Latina Leadership Conference (sponsored by Merrill Lynch), thereby providing an excellent avenue for Merrill Lynch to increase our credibility and visibility within the Hispanic women's market.

"Above all, Nina and I share mutual respect for one another and the desire to see each other succeed. Merrill Lynch is honored to support Nina Vaca and Pinnacle as they grow and prosper."

Chapter Six

Putting it All on Paper: Negotiating the Practical Side of Partnership

WORDS OF WISDOM:
Win-Win Negotiation

"A good deal is one when you do not mind being on either side of the relationship; where you would feel like a winner being on either side."
- Dr. Marsha Firestone, Ph.D.
President, Women Presidents' Organization and Women Presidents' Educational Organization

You have found "The One" with whom you want to partner (or "the ones"—polygamy is okay in business!). You are blissful, energized and excited about your future. You can breathe a huge sigh of relief, but the hard work is far from over. Now comes the planning. Every bride-to-be knows the drill: the engagement ring is barely on your finger and suddenly you are up to your knees in wedding planning! Grooms-to-be find themselves suddenly immersed in tastings, selection of invitations, photographers and caterers, perhaps even a visit to the lawyer to write the "prenup." Business partnership is no different: once you have found your match you still need to jump through a few more hoops to make it all official. Both the bride and the groom need to be prepared to do the homework that will make the wedding a success.

There are no foolproof guarantees, no matter how carefully you set up a business partnership or alliance of any sort, but there are many, many steps you can take to minimize your risk. In this chapter, I have asked trusted experts for advice on negotiating the various and sundry business details of a partnership. While this advice is solid and wide-ranging, every business relationship has its own quirks and nuances, so be sure to access your own network of professional advisors as well.

Taking the Blood Test and Signing the Papers

WORDS OF WISDOM: Get it in Writing

"The most significant mistake you can make is not committing to writing all the components of the partnership and receiving complete, competent legal advice. It can involve significant expense in the start-up phase, but can potentially be a lifesaver down the road."
- WBE Janice Pellar
President, EMCO Technologies, Baton Rouge, Louisiana

I have heard many unmarried but totally committed couples ask the question, "Why is an official piece of paper so important? We know we are devoted to each other." I will opt not to comment on that question when it comes to personal relationships, but in business relationships, a written agreement is absolutely critical. Let me repeat that: "Put it in writing!" You never know what might happen in the future, and you must have a clear record of your responsibilities and the responsibilities of anyone with whom you have an alliance.

The Small Business Administration's Online Women's Business Center offers this wise advice:

"In the excitement of forming your first alliance, you may feel infatuated with your partner and believe that nothing could go wrong with the partnership you are creating. While trust and respect must be present to form a successful alliance, you should also look at the agreement with the jaundiced eye of a jilted lover before you sign any papers, and remember those five building blocks of partnership—timing, financial resources, human capital, support networks and strategic vision. Each of these elements will be present in a strong and comprehensive partnership agreement."*

The SBA lists a few questions, which I have included below, along with my comments and additional issues to consider:

- **Am I comfortable with the time frame of this agreement?** Again, will the time frame work with agreements you have with current clients and vendors? Is the time frame too long or short?
- **Are financial issues discussed in adequate detail? I have done the home work on getting my financial building blocks in place, but what about those of my prospective partner? Are human resource issues discussed in adequate detail?** Do I know exactly how my staff will be affected now and into the future? Are my key employees included in the agreement, if necessary? What about my Board, vendors, suppliers and other important people?
- **What are some of the potential problems of this partnership? From my perspective? From my customers' perspectives?** Always consider the perspective of your clients when reviewing the details of an alliance agreement.

* "Strategic Alliance, Beware the Pitfalls," Online Women's Business Center, www.onlinewbc.gov, 1997.

- **Is this agreement too narrow or too broad?** Will your partnership have room to grow? Does the agreement give your partner too much latitude? Does it meet the needs of your strategic vision and that of your partner?
- **Does this agreement include provisions for resolving conflicts as they occur?** Will a rift in the partnership immediately lead to a lawsuit, or do you have a provision for a mediator or other third-party intervention?
- **How will my/our certification be affected?** What about other networks, such as association memberships, board appointments and Chamber of Commerce dues?
- **Are our mutual responsibilities clearly outlined?** Consider not only what the outline says, but also what that means. Make certain that your new role is something you want.
- **Will this agreement benefit both parties?**
- Remember the win-win-win scenario. If the first two "wins" for your partner and yourself are not solid, your customer will win, but in the long term, the partnership will fail.
- **What is our agreed-upon exit strategy and/or plan for ending this agreement if necessary?**
  Do not rely on what you think will or should happen. At the risk of repeating myself: get it in writing. The same issues are at play when large corporations partner with each other. Consider this "Partnering Checklist" written for the Cisco Systems web site by Andrew B. Whinston and Soon-Yong Choi, coauthors of *The Economics of Electronic Commerce* and *The Internet Economy: Technology and Practice*: *

* "Power from Partnering" by Soon-Yong Choi and Andrew B. Whinston, for Cisco Systems.

A profitable partnership should clearly define how economic benefits are achieved in the following three areas:

- **Coordination Costs:** How easy is it to work collaboratively? Are communication channels and collaborative technologies in place? And are they interoperable? Can workflows be automated? Can common tasks be outsourced?
- **Monitoring Costs:** Is it possible to monitor partner activity? Can the partners report and summarize activities in real time? How will partner communication occur when services are not delivered? Can revenues be analyzed to verify partnership effectiveness?
- **Rules of Sharing:** What are the revenue-sharing rules? Can partners implement such rules in a transparent way? Will partnership efforts lead to a larger share of profits? Will the rules of the partnership foster cooperation?
- Benefits in the current business climate come from separating business processes by specialization, and putting the processes together through partnership. Companies should focus on their core competencies and rely on partners to provide auxiliary services.

Experienced GMEs offer additional suggestions for what you must include in any alliance agreement:

- "Be very, very thoughtful in the discussions and negotaitons and deal as openly as you can with areas that might be conflicts. They sometimes can undermine the relationship. Create the closest possible alignment right from the beginning. [To emphasize this,] I write a preamble to every contract that addresses our intent. For instance, stating why this market will be better

served if we partner, or that 'We will work closely together with sensitivity to one another's issues.'"
- Marilyn Carlson Nelson, CEO, Carlson Companies

- "Clearly define what success means to each partner. Saying you both want 'a great business' is not enough. What geographic areas do you aspire to serve? What exact services will you provide? What are your exact revenue goals? I remember in the heyday of the dot com boom, a major entertainment company partnered with a dot com toy company and in the first year the partnership had revenues of about $50 million. The dot com was thrilled; the major entertainment company thought it was a dismal failure. Clearly they had not defined success at the beginning of their arrangement. Make sure you are on the same page as your partner from the very beginning."
  - Ralph G. Moore, Ralph G. Moore and Associates
- "The ability to end the partnership and a clear understanding of all hidden costs and expectations are an important part of any agreement… It is a mistake to not thoroughly research and have a clear understanding of all requirements of the agreement. You should know what resources will be needed and what costs will be incurred to satisfy the agreement requirements. If seeking a 'partnership for profit,' assure that profit margins are adequate. Always avoid a partnership that cannot be dissolved by either party at any time."
  – Charline Guidry, Chairman and CEO, Diamond Oil Field Supply, Belle Chasse, Louisiana

Let's not forget that the title of this book has a subtitle: Success Strategies for Tomorrow's Supply Chain. The entire idea for this book is based on the premise that the partnership will help to develop and/or maintain a competitive position in increasingly compressed supply chains. Along the path to formalizing a partnership, you must always stay in touch with the ultimate goal: making your company more attractive to your current or potential clients. You may want to do a "trial marriage" as a strategic alliance or team prior to making the final commitment. In any event, be sure your agreement addresses client-related issues and focuses on patterning your behavior in a way that will make you more attractive to corporate buyers with the need to do business with larger, possibly more global companies, whose processes and structures are compatible with their own.

WORDS OF WISDOM

"If you can't pay for a thing, don't buy it. If you can't get paid for it, don't sell it. Do this, and you will have calm and drowsy nights, with all of the good business you have now and none of the bad."
- Benjamin Franklin

JUST-IN-TIME LEARNING: Working with Your Lawyer: A Checklist for Getting an Agreement That Works

Carol Frohlinger, Esq. offers this checklist to GMEs for managing the legal component of your alliance negotiation process:

It is smart business to ignore Shakespeare's line, "The first thing we do, let's kill all the lawyers." Your attorney will play a critical role by documenting the agreement you've struck and ensuring that it is legally enforceable.

Arm your lawyer with the knowledge she needs to represent your interests well, thereby saving yourself time and money in legal costs. Clearly and concisely communicate (preferably in writing) the:

- Correct information regarding the company with whom you will be partnering
    - legal name and form of business entity, i.e. corporation or LLC
    - names and titles of people authorized to legally

bind the company
    - state where the business is organized

- Reasons you want to form this partnership with this company at this stage of your business. For example, "X Company, an industry leader, has distribution channels that will allow my company to increase sales revenue by x percent. We need that growth to meet our business plan targets."
- Reasons your partner wants to form this alliance with your firm at this time. For example, "My company has expertise in ________. X Company doesn't want to develop that capability and has a customer that requires it in the next six months. We have worked with them in the past so they know the quality of the work we do."
- Issues that are important to you about the partnership from a business perspective. For example, "I want to be sure that I get paid on a timely basis." Or, "I need to be assured that my customer list will not be sold to any third parties."
- Things you've learned that are important to your potential partner. For example, "They want to be sure that my company will not subcontract to a third party."
- Issues that you've discussed with your potential partner, particularly if there have been any verbal agreements.

Although following this checklist will take time, it is time well invested. In addition to the usual details, it will provide your lawyer with an understanding of the context for the partnership you wish to form. She will need that background to formulate a strategy for negotiating the legal terms and conditions of the agreement.

Remember too that contracts don't have to be incomprehensible to be legally binding. In fact, agreements that are written in plain English and can be understood by non-lawyers are more likely to be used as a resource to guide the ongoing working relationship between the partnering companies. As such, they tend to avoid lawsuits. Once the contract is drafted, review it carefully and ask about any provision you don't understand.

Finally, consider that the tenor of the contract negotiation will affect your ongoing relationship with your partner. Manage the process carefully by differentiating the role your attorney should play as your legal advisor from your role as the business decision maker.

Carol Frohlinger is a principal in Negotiating Women, Inc. (www.negotiatingwomen.com), a training and consulting firm dedicated to helping women approach negotiation with more confidence and to come away with better results. She is also an author (with Deborah Kolb and Judith Williams) of Her Place at the Table: A Woman's Guide to Negotiating Five Key Challenges to Leadership Success (Jossey-Bass/John Wiley, 2004). She holds a J.D. from Fordham University School of Law.

Staying Certified

How will a strategic alliance impact your current certification? Blanca Robinson, WBENC's Senior Director of Field Operations, explains:

"When two companies decide to form a strategic alliance and thus strengthen their capacity to deliver on a contract to a corporation, careful attention must be paid to the structure of this alliance. If the businesses are to remain as two separate entities, then the businesses can retain their respective certifications. If, however, the alliance itself will be a new business concern, then the new entity should seek certification as a WBE. The certification process for this new entity is the same as for all businesses seeking certification."

Note that the new WBENC certification will be valid for a one-year period.

Clicking

Kelly Lavorgna, head of WBE technology firm MPL Systems, Inc., says that strategic alliances are becoming a necessity rather than an option for her company. According to Kelly, MPL Systems, Inc. was established in 1974 and has successfully created strategic alliances to satisfy many different business objectives for over two decades.

MPL Systems, Inc. is, of course, a technology company and has the luxury of having in-house support for many potential compatibility issues that might arise; but for companies that are not technology based, Kelly offers a checklist of technology-related questions to address.

"When you are aligning with a company, you need to ask the following basic technology questions:

- Do you have an intranet?
- Does everyone have internet access?
- Do you have remote access?
- What kind of network security do you have and at what level?
- Does your company have e-mail?
- Do you have a web site?
- Do you have EDI capabilities?
- What HR software does the company use?
- What type of historical data do you maintain and what type of reports can be generated?

"There are a number of technology tools available that can help alliance companies share information, such as web portals. A web portal allows both companies to share information, collaborate, view status of jobs, and is interactive. These portals basically allow all parties, no matter where they are geographically dispersed, to interact in real-time. Microsoft, for example, has a product called Sharepoint, which allows the users to share and collaborate on documents *http://www.microsoft.com/sharepoint/*.

"Another helpful tool allows the calls from one company to be transferred to another company's phone. The transfer is seamless to the client and is beneficial in instances where you're providing services under one umbrella."

Kelly also recommends that GMEs hire a reputable firm to handle technology issues. "Ask trusted business associates whom they use to maintain their network. Check references and ask questions. Remember, your technology providers, from outside tech support, to your phone company, to your Internet Service Provider, are all partners in your company's success."

Creating a Board of Advisors

As you can see from the above sections, it is very important to access expert advice during the formation of your alliance or partnership arrangement. The more you discuss and clarify your relationship at the outset, the better your chances for success. However, it also important to continue to involve outside experts once your partnership is under way. GME business development expert Ralph G. Moore recommends that partners create a formal or informal advisory board for important partnerships. Who should serve on such an advisory board? Moore defines ideal board members as "people who will make you do some soul searching about how you are doing."

Moore further recommends that advisory boards meet once a quarter, so that partners can step outside the office and talk through issues. "The same questions you answered going into the deal," he says, "are those you need to revisit at least once a quarter. If you start feeling a problem, that quarterly meeting will provide a structure to examine the problem."

If you feel that an advisory board is not the right option for your alliance, it is still a good idea for you and your partner to meet quarterly—away from the daily grind of work—to connect, communicate and deal with problems. On the positive side, regularly stepping away from the office can also result in creative new ideas. I know of one partnership where the two founders meet for their quarterly retreat at a spa where they supplement their business discussions with power yoga!

Another approach is the peer advisory group model offered by the Women Presidents' Organization. The WPO has 48 such groups in the U.S. and Canada as of this writing. Chapters of up to 20 members meet monthly with a professional facilitator and provide a forum for peer group advice and interaction. The WPO's members are a select group of entrepreneurial women presidents who have guided their businesses to generate at least $2 million in gross annual sales. Each local chapter serves as a peer advisory group. The synergy of the group empowers members to achieve increased business and financial success as well as individual growth. They are each partners in one another's progress. As a result, each member exceeds performance expectations for her business and develops a more balanced personal life.

WPO's Platinum Group brings together women from larger companies—revenues of $10 million plus for three meetings a year. This year, WBENC is partnering with the WPO to take this to the next level. For those woman-owned businesses with revenues of $50 million and above, the Zenith Group brings together WPO and WBENC peers from across the country to drive business breakthroughs. Designed for certified entrepreneurial women, the WPO and WBENC will bring together highly motivated, highly successful women in a dynamic forum where they can harness the momentum of their successes and aim for bigger profits and bigger dreams. The group meets twice during the year, once on the East Coast and once on the West Coast. Zenith has two primary objectives:

1. To provide cutting edge information and strategies for successful and fast growth companies.
2. To provide high level business meetings and business development opportunities with Fortune 1000 companies.

A third goal is to assist these firms in developing their own supplier diversity programs that will provide second tier opportunities to smaller GMEs.

PROFITABLE PARNTERSHIP: WPO Branded Roundtable

Founders of fast-growing companies draw upon many sources of knowledge to run their business, from their technical expertise to their interactions with customers. Research has demonstrated that the most invaluable resource to help successful business owners learn and grow is other successful business owners.

As a successful entrepreneur and the inventor of Kitty Litter, Edward Lowe (1920-1995) believed deeply in peer learning as a tool for business owners to share experience and grow as leaders. The Edward Lowe Foundation, whose mission is "to champion the entrepreneurial spirit," has now developed a model to maximize the roundtable experience. That model has been adapted specifically to the needs of the Women Presidents' Organization and will be incorporated into the Zenith Group.

By sharing experiences and gaining support from other entrepreneurs in a confidential roundtable setting, leaders of non-competing businesses benefit from an informal advisory board of smart, thoughtful, dedicated peers. There's a special term for what participants gain in these roundtable discussions: PeerSpective™.

Participants can enhance their leadership and accelerate their personal and business growth in roundtables. They often develop deep friendships with their peers and treat monthly roundtable meetings, and annual retreats, as a chance to step back from workday pressures to see the big picture. Many of the most successful business owners in America attend peer roundtable meetings. Through these lively, educational sessions, participants give and receive the benefit of their entrepreneurial experience, insight and resources under the direction of a trained facilitator.

The typical meeting format begins with a group dinner Thursday evening, followed by a full-day session on Friday with a theme or topic chosen by the members and closes with a half-day session on Saturday that provides enrichment, entertainment or life balance activities. There might be a visiting expert in a particular field, and there is *always* intensive and powerful interaction within this exceptional group of peers. Relationships are strengthened and powerful new bonds are created. In addition to the roundtable experience where mutually important issues are examined, the Zenith Group will provide scheduled meetings to meet decision makers and purchasing officials from the Fortune 1000. Business development meetings will be arranged with these leading corporations to promote new opportunities and may be scheduled throughout the year as well. It is anticipated that formal and informal alliances among the participants will grow from this program.

Are You Changing Your Name?

FedEx Kinko's joined forces and retained both of their strong brand names. UPS bought out Mailboxes, Etc. and decided to eliminate the Mailboxes brand. Other companies merge or partner and form entirely new brand identities Verizon ("can you hear me now?") was created after the merger of GTE and Bell Atlantic (which just a couple of years before this merger had acquired NYNEX). What decision will you make? In business, you must pay attention to your brand as an essential asset. Do not let the brand of your strategic alliance, merger or acquisition be an afterthought.

Here is some additional branding advice from Keith Hines, who headed up the WBENC Board's own branding committee. It is wise counsel for your existing business as well:

- **Think about branding sooner rather than later.** In order to have an effective alliance, people need to know who you are. The brand is the lifeblood of the organization: If people get an inconsistent message, they do not know who you are.
- **Conduct market research.** Test your idea for the alliance's brand. Even though you may not be a large corporation you can still do market research. Try a marketing session with friends and family. Just do not create a brand in a vacuum. Your brand might not click with the public. It needs to be popular and memorable with customers and investors, not just with you. And remember it never hurts to have a catchy name!
- **Keep it simple.** Make sure your brand, logo especially, is easily transferable—not twelve colors and intricate. If you need something more fancy, you can modify your logo later when you are a billionaire!
- **Check before you commit.** Before you go too far with a new brand, make sure the brand does not belong to someone else. Basic trademark searches are relatively inexpensive when you consider the alternative: You could get sued.
- **Think about security.** Once you do settle on a brand that is uniquely yours, police your brand: protect it. Trademark and service mark registration are more costly than a basic search but should also be considered. One more thing in this regard – do not use your

"divorce attorney" to search and register your trademark. This is a specialty and you should hire a firm that specializes in this area. Regularly monitor the security of your brand. These days, doing a web search on a regular basis can be helpful.

- **Know the value of your brand.** A brand can be worth more than the physical sum of the assets of your company. Most corporations are sold, not on the plants and equipment, but on the brand equity. Never underestimate the importance of brand!

Oh My Gosh, We Forgot to Have Children!

No matter how tightly your legal documents have been crafted or how perfectly executed your new logo and web site may be, life happens. Priorities change, clients and customers come and go, economies boom and bust. Keep this in mind as you embark on your new partnership, and keep open your lines of communication. Do not just rely on budgets and legalese to sustain your alliance relationship. Keep that strategic vision top-of-mind.

Like a husband and wife who plan to have children and then become caught up in their careers, you may become so busy with day-to-day issues that you lose track of your long-term goals. Continue to revisit your alliance agreement, financial arrangements, marketing materials and other documents throughout your partnership to stay on your toes and keep your eyes on the future growth of your business.

Just as experts advise business owners to consistently revisit their business plans, I advise you to regularly review your partnership arrangement as you move forward. As in the initial "successful marriage" advice, take time to communicate within the partnership and without. Ask yourself: "Am I continuing to meet the goals of my client or do I need to expand even further by bringing in an additional partner or acquiring capability by buying out or merging with another firm?"

JUST-IN-TIME LEARNING: Your Partnership Registry

Just like a bridal registry that includes kitchen items, china and linens, the beginning of a partnership is a good time to ensure you have a "stocked home" of all the items you will need to make your partnership a success. Here is a checklist, based on the information shared by the experts in this chapter:

- Legal agreement between alliance partners, including a clear exit strategy
- Business plan, including financial goals, of your alliance
- List of customer and/or client prospects
- Clear outline of partner duties and responsibilities
- Official name for strategic alliance (do not forget to check copyrights and trademarks!)
- Web site for strategic alliance
- Marketing materials for strategic alliance
- Board of Advisors or schedule of quarterly partner retreats

Chapter Seven

Making the Most of the Marriage (The See-Saw)

Congratulations! I now pronounce you partner and partner(s). You are official. You have all of the paperwork. You have changed your name, if that is the decision you made. You have made all of your big plans, dreamed of the future and are ready to get on with the rest of your life.

The Honeymoon

There is nothing wrong with enjoying the first flush of happiness and excitement that comes with a new romance. Likewise, I think it is perfectly advisable to start a business partnership with optimism and celebration. The reason you can confidently celebrate your new alliance is because you have diligently covered all of your bases in the previous chapters regarding contingency planning, proper paperwork, human resource management and more. Now you can focus your energy on serving the needs of your clients and creating win-win-win situations.

JUST-IN-TIME LEARNING:
What Makes a Good Marriage?

Here is some advice from GMEs who have enjoyed successful business partnerships:

Be Helpful: "As a partner, our responsibility lies in not only performing our tasks per the contract, but also in making suggestions to improve efficiencies and enhance technical capabilities." Janice Pellar, President, EMCO Technologies, Baton Rouge, Louisiana

Let Yourself Be Helped: "The biggest lesson I got from partnering was learning to receive; to let others help me be successful, to be mentored, and that I do not have to do it alone. This feeds my commitment to do the same for others." Julia Hubbel, President, The Hubbel Group, Lakewood, Colorado

Be Proactive: "Our best business partners reach out to us proactively with new ideas and solutions that help us meet our business goals—they do not wait until there is a problem with the business model or the relationship to reach out to us." Tom Donatelli, Senior Director, Pfizer Global Sourcing

Set Rules from the Start

WBE Sue Romanos of CAREERXCHANGE in Miami, Florida, shares the "Rules of Engagement" she and her two partners developed in addition to their legal agreement. (See the Profitable Partnership profile about CAREERXCHANGE in Chapter Eight.) Consider developing your own guidelines to make sure your partnership runs smoothly.

1. *We agreed to leave our egos at the door and handle each situation as it affects the company, not the individual.*
2. *We respect and love each other. From the outset we said we would deal with each other as if we were dealing with a loved one. We deal with each other as if we were dealing with a loved one. Any disagreements that we have are behind closed doors and never involve employees. At times we agree to disagree, but majority rules. When one partner has a particularly strong opinion about something, we generally support that position.*
3. *Spouses are not permitted to work in the business or be involved in any negotiations. Spouses may share their opin-*

ions at home, but they must stay out of the partnership.

4. *We agreed not to let employees put us on the spot. We avoid the Mommy/Daddy syndrome. Employees know that they cannot go from one owner to another if they do not get the answer they want from the first person they ask. When an owner handles a specific problem with an employee, it is communicated to the other owners so they are aware of what has happened in that particular situation.*
5. *The owners (three shareholders) agree to support each other in front of all employees even if they disagree once a decision is made. We always present a united front.*
6. *Once each year, we review our specific job responsibilities and make adjustments when necessary; the partners have a clear picture of what each is responsible for.*
7. *The partners meet monthly off site to review what we have on our plates. A discussion takes place of what has been accomplished, what is pending and what has been completed.*
8. *The owners meet quarterly with the managers to review where we are in terms of our company goals, team goals and employee-specific goals. Any shortcomings and how to overcome them are discussed at that time.*

Marketing Your New Alliance

Anyone who has ever planned a wedding knows that it can be an all-consuming affair, often becoming like a second full-time job, especially during the last weeks before the big day. Most brides and grooms are quite shocked to learn that the world has gone on while they were planning their nuptials, and the whole world did not, in fact, know about the event.

Business owners planning an alliance can experience the same surprise, feeling shocked that the world—including their own employees, vendors, clients and other important business relationship partners—had no idea. Sometimes, of course, this is deliberate, because partnership discussions often fall through in the negotiation process. Once the deal is sealed, however, your first order of business is to make sure you share the news with your most important constituents, especially the customers who can make your alliance a success.

Just as the bride and groom send out wedding announcements to a broad network of friends and family, the new company should send out a press release announcing the partnership or alliance and its new, expanded capabilities. While that strategy works well for your database, you should write personalized letters to your best customers, and get in touch with your procurement contacts with a list of increased capabilities. Do not forget to merge and purge the databases of the formerly separate companies or you will create the impression that not all of the building blocks have been addressed and merged.

In *Breaking Through,* I included an entire chapter on marketing strategies for certified companies looking to do business with large corporations. All of that information applies to partnerships as well, but alliances need to keep in mind some additional marketing tips:

- **Create new marketing materials.** Do not rely on old marketing materials to tell your new story. Your capabilities are now significantly different, so be sure to communicate them clearly in brochures, presentations, trade show booths and other marketing vehicles. If your alliance involves a new company name, be sure to create a matching logo as well. The WBENC database is an excellent place to look for graphic designers and marketing experts to help you with your new identity.
- **Consider your multicultural marketing efforts as well.** WBENC recently translated its basic WBE

brochure into Spanish. We did this for several reasons. We have a Memorandum of Understanding with the U.S. Hispanic Chamber of Commerce and our Vice President, Linda Denny, serves on their Latina Advisory Council. We are reaching out to Latina businesswomen to join our networks, get certified and become active in our regional women's business organizations. A Spanish language brochure is like a welcome mat that says this is a friendly home and lets your prospective new clients know that you have given thought to their needs and their cultures.

- **Create an online presence for your alliance.** As marketing expert and WBE Nancy Michaels of Impression Impact points out, "Your web site proves your credibility and professional existence. It should explain who you are, what you do, and what others have said about you." You and your partner should consider forming a new web site dedicated to your alliance, or, at the very least, create a clear section on each of your web sites to promote the alliance. Make sure potential and existing customers can easily find information about your services. Not sure if people can find you? Perform a Google search on your name, your partner's name, your company name and the products or services you sell. If you cannot find information on yourself, then customers cannot find you either. If this is the case, web marketing consultants can help make your online presence more visible. As my web-savvy writing collaborator Lindsey Pollak likes to say, "These days, if people cannot find you on the web, you do not exist!"
- **If appropriate, get a second set of business cards.** If you are developing a separate brand for a new strategic alliance that may be temporary or specific to only a niche of your existing business, carry business cards

both for your existing business and for your strategic alliance. Potential customers may become suspicious or confused if you continue to identify yourself as only the head of your original company. By all means, you can incorporate your original business name or logo into the design of your alliance business card, but do not avoid new cards entirely.

- **Do not elope; have a wedding**. Announce your new alliance for the world to hear! Particularly if the alliance involves a name change or name launch, use every communication tool available to spread the word. Make certain that those corporate contacts understand the increased capacity of the firm or alliance to provide value in their supply chain. For the sake of your employees, consider an event—a party, picnic, offsite meeting or even a field trip to your new partner's offices—to include all staff in the alliance relationship.

Seamlessly Serving Your Customers' Needs

Once you have marketed your alliance and begin to win contracts as a team, you must work especially hard to make sure the customer experience is as seamless as when you were the only business involved—this is why you created an alliance in the first place! Ultimately, the most important measure of a successful alliance relationship rests on your effectiveness at responding to the needs of the customers or clients you serve. It is all well and good if you and your alliance partner love to go on vacations together with your families or can chat for hours over cappuccinos, but no partnership can last if your customers are not benefiting.

According to Carol Danoff of Pitney Bowes, focus on promising what you are confident you can deliver and then overdelivering within your alliance and in your contracts. "If you cannot do something, say that you cannot do it," she advises. "If it is going to have to be an investment, commit to that investment together. Things fall apart when people, even big corporate suppliers, claim they have a capability they do not, or claim they can do things that they cannot. Commit only to what you feel very confident you can deliver. People will understand if there are circumstances beyond your control, but do not overpromise, especially at the beginning when you are still building the relationship.

"When suppliers do not perform on a contract, it takes a long time for them to get back in and win other business."

Nancy Williams of ASAP Staffing, agrees. "Delivery is as hard as winning the contract," she says. "You have to have the resources to deliver....We understand a client's goals and objectives from a budgetary standpoint and we steer them into the future and deliver solutions around their problems. Then we make it happen. That is why we are successful with large clients."

Request Feedback

To further ensure that your new alliance is serving your customers' needs, set up an ongoing process for soliciting feedback. WBE Nancy Michaels, quoted above, shares this advice from her book, *Perfecting Your Pitch* (Career Press, 2004):

When I first began my business, I was a bit shy about requesting feedback—both positive and negative—from my clients. Perhaps I was fearful. Now I request feedback every chance I get. I find it the most effective way to continually serve my clients with the kind of service they most desire. I don't think it is ever too early to begin an open dialogue with clients about their satisfaction with your work. Not only will you receive valuable feedback from the get-go, but your clients will also feel valued and listened to. Here are some tips for requesting and analyzing client feedback in the most effective way:

- ***Commit to understanding your client's definition of value – today, tomorrow and forever***

  Knowing what is most important to your client and then delivering on it is your most important job. Because this definition of value is likely to change over time (and perhaps frequently with a difficult client!) due to the ebbs and flows of the business world, you need to constantly reassess your value proposition. Your first articulation of value was in your post-pitch meeting proposal, so use that document as your starting point.
- ***Establish a method of formal client research***

  Depending on the size of your business, you should invest in a trustworthy method of researching your client needs, such as online surveying, which I find to be the most effective method for soliciting both positive and negative feedback.
- ***Continue to solicit informal client research***

  Even when you have implemented a formal means for assessing client satisfaction, you can and should solicit feedback informally as well. For instance, we can all hear it in someone's voice when they are unhappy. Rather than ignoring someone's unpleasant or stressed tone of voice, ASK if anything is wrong and if there is anything you can do to improve your client's situation, whether their dissatisfaction has something to do with you or not. Remember, your goal is not only to provide excellent service to your client for the work you have been hired to perform, but also to serve as a trusted guide and resource in general. Never miss an opportunity to provide service. And, if the problem is related to your work, you want to know sooner rather than later so you can make the appropriate changes to improve your client's satisfaction immediately.

PROFITABLE PARTNERSHIP: LanguageSpeak and ING

One way to increase opportunities by partnering is to create new products that are profitable for both companies. Your client becomes your partner by funding the development or through a contract providing the opportunity for you to fund development of new products and services. LanguageSpeak, headed by Annette Taddeo, followed this formula with ING, one of the company's best clients and partners.

According to Annette, ING had a problem with employees who claimed in their job interviews to speak Spanish, but ended up not speaking the language at the professional level the company needed to serve its clients.

"It was cumbersome for ING to test potential employees," Annette explains, "plus there were legal issues to consider. The testing needed to be done though a vendor that could tell ING if the person was at the level needed. ING needed this process to be easy, quick and customized."

LanguageSpeak responded by creating a first-of-its kind online testing tool called OLA, for Online Language Assessment. They customized the product for ING's needs and the company is now using the tool to test potential employees. As an additional feature, the program lets ING know if a potential employee is not adequately fluent, and how many hours of training they would need to reach that level. This helps the company make decisions about which employees might be worth the investment of additional training.

How did this win-win situation come about? According to Annette, "ING came to me and told me about their issues. We did all of their language translations already, so I proposed the online language testing, which would save them time—they would no longer need to set up and conduct appointments to test language skills, which was a burdensome process for the Human Resources department. Now, online, they literally give the candidate a password and that is it.

"For me it was excellent. I had to make an investment in developing a whole new testing tool, but I loved it because I already knew I had a client to pay for it! It made it easier to go into a whole new area and test it.

"We already had a great relationship with ING so that made it even easier."

Employee Integration

At the outset of this book I emphasized the fact that your employees are crucial partners in the success of your business. But employee relationships and dynamics can change dramatically when you form an alliance with another company. How do you manage the ups and downs of employee relations in your own company and with your partner firm?

According to Nancy Michaels, "Just as you put out a press release to announce your new client relationship to the public, you need to announce the relationship to your employees in a formal, detailed way. While large companies may enjoy the benefit of an internal corporate communications department, smaller companies can follow a similar protocol. You need to educate your employees about their role in the projects to come. This is also an opportunity to share success with your employees. Make them feel part of the excitement that you are no doubt feeling.

"Host an internal company lunch or pizza party to share the details of the new client relationship. This shares your success with everyone in your company and encourages buy-in and loyalty. You will want to provide employees at all levels of your company with the following general information:

- Names, titles and reporting structure of the key employees with whom you will be working. Make sure everyone recognizes these names and understands the function of each person in case they receive a phone call or e-mail from anyone at your partner company.

- An overview of the core business of your alliance partner, particularly if it is a product or service your company has not encountered previously, or if it is a former competitor.
- An overview of the products or services you will be providing together.
- Crucial company changes caused by the new relationship. Change is always a little bit scary, so address any questions or concerns your employees may have. For instance, will you be hiring new staff? Will you be working with new vendors? Will you or any of your staff members be required to travel more frequently? If you do not know the answers to these or other important questions at this point, make note of any employee queries and make a commitment to answer them as soon as you are able.

"Especially if your employees have direct contact with your clients, they must understand all aspects of your alliance and how it affects your product or service and your operations. Make sure your employees are representing your new alliance in the strongest possible way."

Rayona Sharpnack, founder and CEO of the Institute for Women's Leadership, offers additional advice. She has worked extensively with Fortune 500 companies on issues of empowerment, relationship-building, thriving on diversity and being customer-focused. Here are some of her tips to help you manage employees during a partnership:

Q: What are the most common challenges companies face during mergers, acquisitions and alliances?

A: The biggest challenge is the disruption in the "homeostasis" of each company and the effect of that disruption on the employees. Imagine that you received a notice in the mail that another family was going to be moving into your home with you. The two families will now need to jointly decide, who gets which bedrooms, who does what chores, what kind of meals will everyone be eating, what furniture stays and what furniture gets sold off. Mergers and acquisitions similarly wreak havoc with people's lives and stability.

Q: Are there ways to plan for these challenges to lessen difficulties during a merger?

A: You'll want to choose an integration team of both formal and informal leaders from each company. They will be the people who sit down and hash out all these issues and then go back and convince their own constituents why the way it is being done is the best way.

Q: What are your recommendations for managing employee fears and expectations during a partnership of merger?

A: Address the biggest concerns first! People want to know how this is going to affect their compensation, their job security, their job definition, who they report to. Factor in resources (time and money) to help those who are exiting the company. Take good care of them so that the survivors will not feel so much anxiety and the marketplace will continue to respect you.

Q: What leadership skills are important for business owners to master when they are involved in a partnership?

A:

1) Defining and executing equitable division of labor
2) Open-mindedness at what the other sees that you do not see. Be fascinated and curious
3) Regularly giving and receiving feedback about what is working, what is not working and what is missing.

If your partner is a sole proprietor or consultant, you

still need to address issues of integration. According to Marilyn Carlson Nelson, consultants at Carlson Companies have to go through a portion of employee training so they understand the entire culture, what Carlson's values are and what the organization stands for. Again, success relates back to mutual understanding and shared values.

Also remember that employees may fluctuate in their opinions about the partnership, and about the partners, including you. "Like in a marriage," says Roz Alford of ASAP Staffing, "you are going to have good times and bad times with your spouse and children. Even in the good times, it is like a marriage; sometimes you do not like your spouse and sometimes you do not like your partner! Sometimes your children go back and forth from one parent to another just like your employees go back and forth from partner to partner."

PROFITABLE PARTNERSHIP: Victory Personnel Services and Manpower

Kathy Greco, Director of Supplier Diversity at Manpower Professional, shares another partnership success story:

Victory Personnel Services Inc., Milwaukee's first African American-owned temporary employment agency targeting central-city job seekers, opened its doors in 1991. Today, Founder and President Joe Tucker and his staff provide some of Milwaukee's largest companies with a diverse pool of professional, administrative and clerical candidates.

Tucker's success is evidenced by a long list of awards. He was named Minority Supplier of the Year by the Wisconsin Minority Supplier Development Council in 2002. He was also part of the Metropolitan Milwaukee Association of Commerce's Future 50 program for fast-growing companies in Milwaukee. And in 1994, Ernst & Young named him Entrepreneur of the Year for the State of Wisconsin.

Since the company's beginnings, Victory has grown steadily

in the Milwaukee market. In the late 1990s, Manpower's Milwaukee staffing office tapped Victory Personnel as its diversity supplier for a major local account. The experience was very positive for both companies, and they continued to work together on other local accounts and cultivated a strong base of customers over a five-year period.

"Because Joe has very similar business practices and goals, he became my first-choice diversity supplier," says Anne Edmunds, director of Manpower's Chicago region. Edmunds oversaw Manpower's business in the Milwaukee area when the company began working with Victory Personnel. "We have built a positive relationship based on trust and communication. We are very successful when we work together."

As a member of the CEO Supplier Diversity Task Force, Tucker found he crossed paths with Manpower again, but at the corporate level. Kathy Greco was active on the task force and was impressed with Tucker's knowledge of the staffing industry.

"Joe is dedicated and driven to making his own business successful and furthering other minority-owned businesses," says Greco. "I respect what he has already accomplished, as well as his ambitious business goals."

As a key leader in Manpower's Diversity Supplier Mentoring Partnership Program, Greco believed Tucker had the qualities Manpower seeks in its diversity suppliers. Having learned that Tucker was very interested in expanding Victory Personnel outside of Milwaukee and Wisconsin, she encouraged him to consider the program.

"My customer niche is large, Fortune 500-type companies. My experience with that caliber of customer was attractive to Manpower," explains Tucker. "The partnership program appealed to me because I want to learn and make my business better. This was an opportunity to study with the industry leader."

Tucker was accepted into Manpower's program, which offers a mix of mentoring, partnership and internship programs.

Shortly after that, a business opportunity presented itself. Manpower's diversity supplier for a customer in the pharmaceutical industry closed its doors, and Manpower was seeking a new partner. Aware of Tucker's interest in expanding his operations, Manpower asked if he would be interested in launching a new office in the Chicago suburbs to service the pharmaceutical customer as well as another major national account in the communications industry.

Within one week, Tucker was able to secure an office, hire an employee and complete the on-boarding process with the temporary employees from the former diversity supplier. In fact, the employees never missed a paycheck.

"Joe really went the extra mile in this situation and proved himself yet again," raves Greco. "The resourcefulness he exhibited affirms our decisions to partner with Victory Personnel, and we look forward to partnering in other markets as we present opportunities to each other."

Chapter Eight

Marriage Counseling

The stated purpose of this book is to help you create and sustain profitable partnerships in order to increase your business with corporations and other customers. We hope that will be the result of reading this book and following the advice and recommendations. However, we all know that everything is not always perfect. No matter how balanced we all try to keep our see-saws, sometimes partnerships feel more like roller coasters. Even the most committed, successful and profitable partnerships have their ups and downs. Sometimes these challenges can strengthen the partnership, and other times they can lead us to throw in the towel. This chapter addresses some of the problems that partners can face, and provides counsel on negotiating the hard times and, if necessary, the break-up.

Buyer's and Seller's Regret

I am confident that if you have read this far and followed the advice from various experts and experienced GMEs, you will not find yourself in a situation of feeling buyer's or seller's regret. Sometimes this regret comes from allowing outsiders to convince you to pursue a course of action that does not feel right to you. I recently met one WBE who sold her company and has regretted it ever since. "It was my one big idea," she confided, "and I gave it away."

The best way to avoid regret is to pay close attention to your instincts and consult with the mentors and business advisors you most trust.

Anticipate and Address Problems

Chapter Six included a recommendation to form an advisory board and/or to hold quarterly meetings with your partner to create a forum for addressing problems or concerns in your relationship. This is an important strategy, but sometimes issues arise that must be dealt with immediately. It is my policy to address issues sooner rather than later and not to brush problems under the rug and hope they will disappear. It is not easy to confront someone—particularly a business partner; however, if you are uncomfortable with confrontation, I have one piece of advice for you: Confrontation is never fun, but bankruptcy is worse.

One positive way to address conflict is to turn adversities into opportunities. I had a client in my AWED days who manufactured designer chocolates. She had an elegant company name for her elegant product. As she grew her business, she ended up entering into a contract with a mass merchandiser to knock off her own product. In the process of negotiating, she could see that the large company did not respect her and her brand and they did not see her as an equal. Instead of giving in to their demands or running away from the lucrative deal, she instead decided to negotiate with the mass merchandiser to agree to let her market cheaper products under a different name from that of her luxury products.

Troubleshooting

Where can you turn for help, suggestions and ideas if your partnership appears to be going south? Here are some steps to take:

1. Assess the problem and communicate.

According to the supplier diversity professionals and business owners I interviewed, the most common problems include the following. If any of these are at issue in your situation, think about the following questions when assessing your problems:

- **Control.** Are you conflicted over where the buck ultimately stops? Was this determined at the beginning of your partnership and now needs to be reassessed?
- **Human resources.** Are you arguing about certain employees, key staff in particular? Are you dealing with cultural issues stemming from the interaction between two formerly independent entities?
- **Vendor relationships**. Are you at odds about what firms to use for key business relationships?
- **Client relationships and service.** Are you in disagreement about how to manage a certain client, contract or project? Does one of you have a better relationship with the client? Remember that your customers or clients must remain top-of-mind no matter what your issues with your alliance partner, so be careful not to reveal your problems in an inappropriate situation like a meeting or site visit.

JUST-IN-TIME LEARNING: What if my partner changes into another person...literally?

As WBE Ellie Halter, CEO of Schnipke Engraving Co., points out, communication is especially essential when the players change in your partnership arrangement. If you are working in an alliance with a larger company, your original contact or day-to-day "partner" may leave the company. Halter says, "Always remember that a change in ownership or management of that partner may not extend to the new management, so you need to be on guard for this and try then to nurture the new relationship."

This is another good reason to forge strong relationships with many employees at your partner or alliance company, and to have airtight legal arrangements. Do not let your entire partnership rest on your relationship with a single person.

2. Consult an unbiased third party for assistance.

Many people associate the field of mediation with marriage—when couples considering divorce seek to solve their issues through a friendly mediator rather than adversarial lawyers. Mediators are also becoming common in business relationships. Some mediators are lawyers, but many are not (some are even psychologists by training). According to independent business consultant Ronnie Feit, mediators do not give "answers." Rather, they help partners work together to develop agreements tailored to meet their unique needs. Some partnership contracts require that, in the event of conflict, partners participate in mediation prior to seeking a binding decision through either arbitration or the traditional court process.

What are the pros and cons of mediation? According to Ronnie, since the parties control the outcome in mediation, the cost and length of the process is not entirely predictable. Generally, however, it is less expensive and faster than going to court. Similarly, there is no guarantee that mediation will resolve the dispute. Unlike in arbitration and court, resolution depends on the parties' willingness to agree, not on a third party's ability to dictate a decision.

Most parties who participate in mediation are satisfied with the process, independent of the outcome. Satisfaction is related to a number of issues, among them the opportunities to be heard, to preserve relationships and to control the outcome. In mediation, parties can express concerns about *all* issues they consider important, not just those pertaining to legal rights and obligations. Adversarial processes almost invariably damage relationships, both business and personal. Mediation, on the other hand, is a collaborative process, increasing the chances that the parties will view each other as co-problem solvers, not "the problem." Finally, since agreements reached through mediation are created by the parties, compliance rates are higher than when decisions are rendered by a third party.

Those considering mediation should compare the potential costs of mediation with those of arbitration and litigation—financial, emotional, productivity-wise and others. They should also ask themselves a few key questions including: "How important is it that I retain control of the outcome?" and "How important is my relationship with my partner, either within the partnership or in potential business or personal interactions, should we decide to end the partnership?" And, if the answer to either of these questions is yes, it is probably worth finding out more about your mediation options.

If you are interested in learning more about mediation or finding a mediator, visit the Association for Conflict Resolution web site (*www.acresolution.org*), which is a nonprofit organization whose mediators resolve a wide range of disputes through mediation and other dispute resolution processes. Note that, as of yet, there is no one national certification for mediators, so Ronnie recommends performing extensive due diligence and reference checks before hiring a mediator.

Another way to address issues of conflict in your partnership—or any business issues, for that matter—is to join a peer networking group such as the Women Presidents' Organization, which has chapters in cities across the United States and in Canada. Many members work through partnership dilemmas at their WPO meetings, says President Marsha Firestone. "It gives them a forum to talk about their own experiences with the input and support of others who have had similar experiences."

3. Consult a biased third party for assistance.

In some cases, such as a strategic alliance or joint venture constructed in order to service the needs of a large corporate client, it may help to involve the supplier diversity professional who helped you win the business. Be sure you are clearheaded and professional about your disagreement, as you do not want to cause your customer concern that the problem may hurt your ability to carry out your contract. But know that the supplier diversity executive wants to help. It is in his or her best interest, of course, to make sure that your alliance is functional and thriving.

Bruce Perkins of Merrill Lynch says that suppliers come to him when they are experiencing problems. His strategy is to serve as a gatherer of potential solutions rather than an all-knowing problem solver: "I get involved and I ask them to tell me the issues," he says, "and then I think about it and review my literature and research possible solutions. I also call some of my mentors and get some suggestions. Then I meet with them again and offer my advice. I tell them it's coming from various sources and then give them my 'uniform assessment.'"

When to Call it Quits: Exiting Gracefully

Sonny and Cher. Brad Pitt and Jennifer Aniston. Even Barbie and Ken. The sad reality is that sometimes relationships just do not work out. From disagreements, to separation, to divorce, life happens and some partnerships, even those started with the best of intentions, are just not meant to be. Ralph Moore calls it "the moment of truth—when you know it is not going to get better." Sometimes it is better to end a relationship than to keep trying to save it. "It is like spoiled milk," Ralph describes. "You do not put it back in the refrigerator and hope it gets better."

Of course, as Ralph acknowledges, "It takes courage to pull the plug. You have to be very decisive." But, as I said earlier, it is better to have the difficult conversation than to end up failing a customer or losing your company.

Remember that ending a partnership, or exiting your own business, can be a very positive move. As we addressed earlier in the book, exit strategies are an important component of any strategic plan.

WBE Patricia Henriquez, whose stories have appeared throughout this book, knew that she needed to develop an exit strategy for her company and wanted to end on a positive, profitable note. She did not have children to whom she wanted to pass the business and she did not want to work forever, so she looked at the alternatives. Fortunately, she had a board of directors that worked in partnership with her to evaluate the options—sell, take in a partner, or do an ESOP (Employee Stock Ownership Plan)—and then come up with a strategy for the agreed upon plan. In 1995, Pat and her board decided that she would ultimately sell her company and so spent the next five years carrying out the plan they devised to make the company attractive and valuable to a purchaser. That included strengthening her government practice and expanding the firm's reputation nationally. The strategy worked and she successfully sold her company.

As you think about ways your own partnership may develop and possibly come to an end, once again I recall the building blocks of partnership:

- Is now the right time to dismantle this alliance?
- What are the financial ramifications (positive or negative) for our companies?
- How will ending this relationship affect our employees?
- Am I consulting the right personal and professional advisors during this process?
- How does ending this relationship fit into my strategic vision for the future?

As you can see, sometimes ending a partnership is just as much a win-win-win as beginning one. The reality is that throughout one's life and the life of one's company, many partnerships begin and end. But if you pay attention to your building blocks and make smart decisions that also pass your own personal "gut check," partnership will ultimately be a positive, profitable experience for all involved.

PROFITABLE PARTNERSHIP: CAREERXCHANGE

The partners in CAREERXCHANGE know a lot about the connection between marriage and business—they met through their friendship as married couples! Sue Romanos, current President of WBENC-certified CAREERXCHANGE of Miami, Florida, had a successful career in the staffing industry and, prior to that, in the securities industry in New York City. She and her husband, Ted, became friends with Suzanne Hodes' husband, Gerry, when they all worked at the same securities firm in New York in 1962. In 1978 when Suzanne met her husband, he introduced her to Sue and Ted. Throughout the years, the couples saw each other three to four times a year and spoke frequently in between.

Sue began thinking about starting a business of her own but for various reasons it just didn't seem to work out. During this time Suzanne quit her job and had a child. When she was ready to go back to work full-time, Sue suggested she try the staffing industry. Suzanne took the advice and went to work for an executive recruiting firm in Miami. Less than a year later, in 1988, Sue and Suzanne began talking about the idea of going into the recruiting business together.

According to Suzanne, "We discussed every possible scenario under the sun and then sought the advice of an attorney. We told him what we wanted to do and how we wanted to accomplish it. We asked him for guidelines how to accomplish this. He told us that starting a new company and working together side by side 40 to 60 hours a week was just like getting married. He came up with a slew of questions that we hadn't even thought of. We went back and hashed out the questions. We figured out how we would 'get married' and, if necessary, divorced, and wrote this into our agreement.

"We opened our doors the first week in January 1989. During the subsequent years we grew steadily and became very active in our community and within our industry. We made it a point to create strategic alliances with some local competitors and even became friends with a few. In 1997, Nick Alonso, owner of Contemporary Personnel, approached us about a possible merger. He was one our local competitors with whom we had a strategic alliance. I always make the remark that we dated from 1989 through 1997 and had our second marriage in 1997! Since 1997, we have acquired the client accounts of two other local competitors that went out of business. We have grown our business through organic growth and acquisitions from zero to $11.2 million dollars by the end of 2004."

Chapter Nine

Partnerships of the Future

I began this book by sharing my light bulb moment at the Ford-hosted Billion Dollar Roundtable meeting I attended a few years ago. Learning of the trend that corporate supply chains were compressing, I helped steer WBENC and our certified WBEs in the direction of strategic alliances, joint ventures, partnerships and everything else you have been reading about. As we have emphasized throughout this book, the purpose of the strategy of partnership is to sustain and grow your competitive stance in the corporate supply chain.

As we come to the end of our discussion of partnership, the next question is: What else is just over the horizon that will affect business processes and supply chain dynamics in the days and years ahead? This chapter offers an overview of my newest "light bulbs" and some of the "whispers" others are hearing around the supplier diversity industry.

Wider-Reaching Certification

As I have mentioned, WBENC partners with numerous other organizations to carry out our mission and expand our reach to serve the needs of our various constituents. One growing trend in the certification field is partnerships between private certification, like WBENC, and government certification. In the past, GMEs often had to go through the lenghty certification processes of various towns, states and industries with which they wanted to do business. Increasingly, government procurement officials are recognizing WBENC certification and using that to expedite a WBE's application for some government certifications. This "partnership" of WBENC and government agencies helps open more doors for GMEs.

Innovation in the Energy Industry

Increasingly, like-minded people who recognize the value of supply chain diversity are working together to facilitate the inclusion of GMEs. One example comes from the energy industry, where a vision of a future with reduced energy marketplace impediments for Women and Minority Business Enterprises (WMBEs) has led to some exciting new strategies.

Starting in 1994 with an MOU (Memorandum of Understanding) signed by 21 major energy companies, WMBEs, banks and agencies, there has been an ongoing effort to level the playing field in this industry. Recognizing that many WMBE businesses were underutilized and undercapitalized, Sempra Energy, Chevron, Amoco and Union Bank created the *Funds Transfer Agent Agreement* (FTAA) to facilitate WMBE gas deals. Soon after, the U.S. Department of Energy got involved and adapted the FTAA for nationwide use. Federal Reserve Banks began to give banks credits for the use of FTAA, which helped finance the purchase of gas contracts that were resold for a profit by a WMBE.

In 2001, the National Association of Regulatory Utility Commissioners (NARUC) became a partner in the effort by unanimously approving the program renamed the *Natural Gas Market Access Program for WMBEs*. They developed policies and principles that guided the efforts to drive greater utilization and inclusion and within a few years had identified issues, constraints and barriers that WMBE companies faced in the marketplace. A national supplier diversity resolution was passed and adopted.

In 2004, the focus expanded beyond the gas markets to include electricity, water and telecommunication sectors and the procurement of all goods and services provided to utility companies. To reflect this change, the name was updated to *the Utility Market Access Partnership*. Service disabled veterans enterprises were included with women and minority business enterprise (WMBEs) and the group was renamed Diverse Business Enterprises (DBEs). I like this definition of DBE far better that the standard "D" for disadvantaged. Model Market Access Standards were developed to encourage state utility commissions and utility companies to voluntarily adopt the Standards and maximize opportunities for DBEs. New generations of like-minded people are actively working to implement the voluntary standards by having state utility commissions and utility companies adopt the standards, which require them to set and report numerical goals for doing business with DBEs. They are encouraging utilities to place subcontracting language in all product, service and construction contracts over a certain dollar amount.

Certification as a women's business enterprise, minority business enterprise or as a service disabled veteran is necessary in order to be part of these programs. WBENC certification is preferred for WBEs and NMSDC certification for MBEs. Service Disabled Veterans can be certified by the Small Business Administration or the Association for Service Disabled Veterans Businesses or by other groups approved by the state.

WBENC is playing an active role as a new partner in this long-term, ongoing effort to build opportunities in a marketplace where few had existed before. Such partnerships of the future will often evolve, based on solid work of the past, to include new groups of people who can help such a project gain momentum and move forward.

Innovation in Local Government Certicification

Another example involves the New York City Department of Small Business Services (SBS), which has partnered with WBENC's New York certification affiliate, the Women Presidents' Educational Organization (WPEO). Here is a description of this program, provided by Glenis Henriquez, Director of External Affairs for the Department:

"We are extremely proud of joining WPEO in an unprecedented certification partnership. What this marriage means to woman-owned businesses is that after certifying with WPEO, they can solicit New York City certification in an expedited way. Without WPEO certification, a business would need to go through the conventional certification application (over 30 pages long). The newly created Fast Track application is two pages long. It presents the woman business owner with an easier method of obtaining city certification. (And we all like 'easy'!

"However, the most important part of this blending of WPEO and NYC SBS is that the members of WPEO, once certified with SBS, will be 'at the table' for city contracts—that is amazing! WPEO's members are privy to private procurement activities (procurement activities of Fortune 100 companies). But now, once certified with NYC SBS, the circle of procurement opportunity is widened to include city contracts. "It is important to recognize that this marriage was only possible through the leadership of WPEO's Marsha Firestone. She should be commended for her vision to reach farther than most in order to create additional contracting opportunities for her WPEO members."

Geri Swift, President of the Women's Business Development Center, whose Women's Business Enterprise Council is WBENC's affiliate in Pennsylvania, Delaware and Southern New Jersey, has experienced similar success with gaining acceptance of

WBENC certification in both Delaware and Pennsylvania. The State of Delaware launched an office of minority and women's enterprise in 2001. In January, 2002, they started a certification process and sought ways to increase the number of certified businesses. Mary Ann Schreiber, Executive Director of that office, had met Geri through networking at small business-focused events. As part of a strategy to streamline their process, they began accepting WBENC certification at a time when they had no process of their own and no registry of certified businesses. Representatives of the state program have attended the last two WBDC conferences and participated in workshops on doing business with state government.

The Pennsylvania experience is another endorsement of both networking and becoming involved in public affairs. Geri has always been active in local and state public policy matters as these affect both support for her organization as well as for its WBE clients. The current governor of the state, Edward G. Rendell, had previously been mayor of Philadelphia and Geri had served on his small business advisory council. Geri explains, "We had a relationship. I served on the Governor's transition team and in one of my papers wrote of the need for the state government to look at the private sector's best practices, especially in the area of supply chain management. Donald T. Cunningham, Secretary of the General Services Administration, moved this agenda ahead and chaired the Governor's Advisory Committee on Minority and Women Business Opportunities. We met on this issue with our council members, and the Secretary asked us to pull together a group of WBEs from across the state—those that had done business with the state and those that hadn't—so that he could form a clear picture of the challenges of doing business and getting certified."

As a result of their discussions, Geri Swift, five WBENC-certified women's business enterprises and Tim Krenz from UPS were appointed to serve on the Governor's Advisory Committee.

According to Geri, "Secretary Cunningham realized that the state's certification and procurement policy and procedures needed reform, and he wanted to implement a strategic sourcing initiative with the mutual goals of cost reduction and efficiency and inclusion of minority and women's business enterprises. To open the doors of opportunity to more women and minority owned businesses, Cunningham worked to have the state accept WBENC and NMSDC certification for Pennsylvania businesses with 100 employees or fewer. He is committed to removing two barriers: the Home State Rule that limits the program to Pennsylvania-based businesses and the 100-employee limit."

Benefits are already being seen by GME firms. Joanne Harmelin, CEO of media buying company Harmelin Media, recently was awarded, as part of the governor's strategic sourcing initiative, 100 percent of Pennsylvania's media buying contract. This is the largest media buying contract the state has ever awarded!

Geri reports that New Jersey is not far behind and that both she and Marsha Firestone, whose WPEO covers the northern part of the state, are applying pressure for the acceptance of WBENC certification.

It's a Small World, After All: Increasing Globalization

In another "whisper" of future trends in the supplier diversity realm, I am hearing an increasing demand from WBENC's corporate members to expand our own activities on a more global basis. These companies want to carry their domestic supplier diversity programs across borders and overseas. At first, I wanted to ignore this problem because we have not yet climbed every mountain here in the United States for WBEs. There is still an enormous disparity between the number of woman-owned firms and their access to major corporate and government contracts, the type of contracts that allow growth and provide opportunities to expand employment and create wealth. But, our corporate members *are* our partners and we need to meet their changing needs as well as those of WBEs. They want to copy what the U.S. has done with WBENC in the other countries in which they do business.

The Future of Purchasing and Supply

A comprehensive literature search was performed by A.T. Kearney to identify materials relevant to future trends that may affect how business will be conducted over the next 10 years. These trends, which include: the expectations, acceptance and demand of change; democratization and capitalization; technology; a global economy; a larger and more diverse population; an aging population; and improvements in worker skills and education, are likely to have an impact on purchasing and supply in the following ways:

- Regional and global sourcing strategies will become a critically important source of competitive advantage;
- The number of key suppliers to firms will be reduced to maximize leverage on a global basis. Suppliers' regional and global capability expectations will increase;
- Strategies and tactical sourcing work will be further separated;
- Executive management expectations of purchasing/supply will increase due to the cross-functional, cross-boundary emphasis and focus on alliances with both suppliers and customers;
- Purchasing/supply will be increasingly integrated with the strategic plans of the firm to maximize company-wide leverage;
- Purchasing/supply performance measures will become further aligned with company wide measurements;

- Information systems/technology will be key to globalization and sourcing strategies enterprise wide;
- New, more complex skills and focus will be required in purchasing/supply to operate in a globally complex and uncertain world; and
- More flexibility and external customer focus will be required in purchasing/supply activities to maximize supplier contributions.

(Center for Advanced Purchasing Studies, National Association of Purchasing Management, A.T. Kearney, Inc. 1998. The Future of Purchasing and Supply: A Five- and Ten-Year Forecast.)

The NMSDC has forged the way once again and assisted organizations in Brazil and England to establish diversity programs. The automotive industry has spearheaded programs for Aboriginal populations in Canada and several WBENC corporate members—Merrill Lynch, Morgan Stanley, HP and IBM—are working with the European Union's Migration Policy Group to establish pilot programs for supplier diversity.

In the U.S., many women's business organizations have created successful formal and informal partnerships overseas. We never cross into each other's territory—we have well-defined spaces, but we are always aware of one another's capabilities, projects and plans. Many organizations have begun to follow a similar model in identifying women's business organization partners across the globe. Many WBENC corporate members who are international companies look to us to identify appropriate partners for their overseas procurement programs. As one example, the government of Canada established a Prime Minister's Task Force on Women's Entrepreneurship in 2003 that traveled to the U.S. to interview leaders in the women's business community.

A leader in this field is Virginia Littlejohn, the founder and CEO of Quantum Leaps, Inc. Virginia worked with OECD

(Organization for Economic Cooperation and Development) in 2003-2004 to coordinate a global women's conference in Istanbul in conjunction with the Ministerial Meeting on SMEs (small and medium sized enterprises). In conjunction with the OECD meeting, IBM sponsored *Accelerating Women's Entrepreneurship* that provided a meeting ground for women business leaders from across the globe. Some of us in the women's organization community, including Terry Neese of WIPP, Marsha Firestone of the WPO and myself, for example, were part of the official U.S. delegation and participated in the ministerial meetings.

The chair of the delegation was then SBA Deputy Administrator Melanie Sabelhaus, who had several opportunities to address the delegates. An inspiring speech was delivered by Marilyn Carlson Nelson. Others, like Ann Marie Almeida of the Association of Women's Business Centers, WBEs Carmen Castillo (SDI) and Himanshu Bhatia (Rose International) and WBENC Board Chair Joan Kerr of SBC Communications, attended the ministerial meetings as visitors and then participated in the post-meeting women's conference. IBM, whose Vice President Theo Fletcher is eager to spread the company's diversity programs throughout its global footprint, brought in several of its women executives from the U.S. and elsewhere in their world-wide operations.

Javette Jenkins, who at that time headed up IBM's supplier diversity program and served on the WBENC Board of Directors, was delighted with IBM's participation and that the value of the contacts and networks that the U.S. women were developing abroad was also helping IBM. She told me at the event, "We have been trying to get to the right people around the world and identify the organizations to work with—and they are all in this room!" The Ministry of Commerce in Turkey was also impressed with both the conference and with Virginia Littlejohn's vast knowledge of the global women's business community—

and has hired her to establish programs in that country to advance opportunities for women entrepreneurs. The OECD is taking its commitment to a higher level as well and will be working to extend the progress made at this meeting, also with Virginia's advice and involvement.

A challenge that has been identified in trying to replicate programs like WBENC's abroad, is the lack of census data on business ownership by women and minorities. (We often take for granted and do not appreciate the value provided to advocates and policy makers alike of the data provided by the Census Bureau.) No data exists on the percentages of contracts, either in terms of revenue or number of contracts, going to these firms from corporations or government entities. No definitions of what constitutes a woman- or minority-owned company are codified in law or regulation. It is difficult to make a business case for the greater inclusion of previously excluded groups if the problem has been rendered invisible by virtue of a lack of verifiable data. An important outcome of the OECD Ministerial meeting's final report was the inclusion of a recommendation that member countries begin to collect data that will form a base line for building a business case for supplier diversity programs.

An important question for the WBENC network will be: What role will American WBEs play in this global expansion? Will the expansion of supplier diversity across borders provide opportunities for new strategic alliances and global partnerships of woman-owned businesses with similar goals and compatible products and services? What role will certification play in the new business model and what organization will provide that certification? I am frequently asked by businesses in Canada and elsewhere to bring our certification to their country. Unfortunately, it is not that simple. The WBENC certification is based on U.S. laws, regulations and history that are not really exportable. Each country is different and while some of the basics—51 percent ownership, management and control, for instance, might be the same, other factors such as tax laws and incorporation requirements will differ. A short-term, perhaps more practical approach to be explored would be identifying ways in which existing WBE suppliers can assist both their corporate client and that client's offshore supplier.

Joan Kerr, Executive Director of Supplier Diversity for SBC and chair of the WBENC board has launched a new Global Business Committee for WBENC. According to Joan:

"There is no doubt that WBEs must grow in order to remain first tier suppliers to large corporations. However, equally important is that WBEs and WBE advocates assess the impact of the globalization of corporate supply chains. The issue is not just, 'Does my corporate customer do business internationally?' or 'Do they have international customers?' or even, 'Do I as a WBE want international customers?' The question is: 'Do the supply chains of my current corporate customers reach offshore?' Increasingly the answer from every corporation is 'YES!'

"The imperative to lower costs and create the greatest efficiencies requires any procurement organization to consider the relative value of offshoring in at least some part of the supply chain. Any company that is buying or producing manufactured goods has already addressed this issue. Any company that procures IT services or develops software as part of their products and services has addressed this issue. Sophisticated procurement processes are a strategic imperative and a competitive advantage. A 'best shore' evaluation should be part of any cost analysis of a supply chain and WBEs need to determine if their products and services can be improved or costs lowered by working with offshore suppliers and partners as well.

"In addition, the growth of global economies opens up opportunities for partnering with businesses around the globe. WBEs may find that their domestic marketing skills and customer base would be highly valuable to an offshore partner.

WBEs may find that they can be more competitive in their domestic business by working with lower cost offshore partners. A great example of this is Argent Associates, a WBENC-certified firm owned by Beatriz [Betty] Manetta, which has formed a successful alliance with a South African-owned company that repairs telecommunications circuit packs. Argent is well positioned as a supplier to the U.S. telecom market and that market needs circuit pack repairs. However, the telecom industry is seeking lower costs in every aspect of its supply chain, and only by forming an offshore alliance could Argent bring domestic customers the cost structure they needed. Argent's South African partner did not have the U.S. customers and the U.S. telecom industry knowledge that Manetta was able to bring to the table. Clearly, there were wonderful advantages to be realized by both partners and by customers too in this global supply chain.

"[Another example, featured earlier in this book,] Rose International was exclusively a U.S. domestic operation until its U.S. customers made it clear that they were seeking 'best shore' IT solutions. Rose did not take long to figure out that by establishing an Indian-based branch of their business they would improve their competitive position and without such a solution, their business would increasingly be vulnerable to competitors with such cost advantages. Rose now has a 500-person operation in Delhi that has allowed it to compete head to head with large Indian IT companies and well-known U.S. based consulting firms with operations in India."

Solidifying Second Tier

We have come full circle from the light bulb moment that started this book. Recently, Ford Motor Company announced the launch of a new diversity reporting system, named M-tier. The M-tier system ("M" stands for multi) is designed to identify and track purchases from diverse suppliers throughout Ford's supply chain. While many companies have struggled and still struggle with insuring that their second tier programs have teeth, the automotive industry is leading the way to make certain that diverse suppliers even at the fourth tier, fifth tier and further down are counted and that the spend is monitored throughout the supply chain.

The growth of WBE firms in the WBENC network has been phenomenal with a strong and growing portfolio of companies with revenues in excess of $50 million per year. These larger women owned firms are starting or expanding their own supplier diversity programs, and WBENC is helping with programs like Zenith, which I discussed at several points throughout the book. Even at the $10 million to $20 million level, WBEs are increasingly setting the bar for the integration of supplier diversity in their own business processes.

Supply Chain Management— Ongoing Challenges

WBEs are not alone in their concern about the future. Corporations are actively looking at policies that will help them to maintain diversity in the supply chain as business processes continue to evolve. In 2002, two major projects were undertaken in the telecom industry that have implications and relevance for all industries. The first was a Blue Ribbon Task Force convened by SBC Communications that focused on maintaining a diverse supply base and supporting existing suppliers during a major industry down turn. The second was undertaken by the Telecom Supplier Diversity Task Force (TSDTF) whose complete report can be found at the NMSDC learning portal (*www.nmsdcus.org*). WBENC's newly formed Strategic Sourcing and Supply Chain Effectiveness Committee looked at these reports as a starting point for its own review and recommendations. They narrowed the TSDTF's 21 recommendations down to just five key areas to be addressed by WBENC. See the sidebar for a summary of these recommendations, which will surely affect all WBENC-certified businesses in the future.

Summary of Recommendations of WBENC Supply Chain Sub-committee

Having reviewed and discussed the 21 recommendations of the TSDTF, we suggest that five Key Recommendations be adopted by WBENC, as follows:
WBENC Corporate Members, whose total revenues exceed a specified annual value, should demonstrate steady and deliberate progress toward compliance with the following:

1. Integrated Supplier Diversity Strategy: Procurement Management and General Management should develop, document, and deploy an integrated Supplier Diversity (SD) strategy. The depth and breadth of such a strategy is outlined in the attached.

2. Aligned Procurement and Marketing SD Strategies: Procurement Management should work with Sales & Marketing Management to ensure alignment and communication of the Supplier Diversity business case, especially as it relates to Sales and Marketing objectives, strategies, and tactic. Supplier Diversity programs must have full support from across the entire organization.

3. SD Access Embedded in Procurement Processes: Procurement Management should integrate Supplier Diversity access and consideration into documented procurement processes, including strategic sourcing and routine buying processes. Typical process steps are outlined in the attached.

4. A Tier 2 Program: Procurement Management should incorporate Supplier Diversity requirements into their prime contracts above a specified value, i.e. "In scope" Corporations should execute a Tier 2 policy.

5. Support for SD Leadership Development Programs: Procurement and General Management should actively support, and participate in, Supplier Diversity Leadership programs including mentoring, educational and/or other development programs specifically targeting Leadership, General, and Financial Management.

Furthermore, if these recommendations are adopted, WBENC will communicate these expectations and, at least yearly, conduct a self-assessment survey of the level of compliance and improvement in this important area.

Why Only Five Recommendations from the 21 Original?
This sub-committee agreed that it would be prudent to adopt a limited number of high priority recommendations, and drive them to adoption, rather than propose a basket of best practices on a share-and-adopt-if-you-wish basis.
Furthermore, the TSDTF was, appropriately, focused on the specific needs of the Telecom Industry, their diverse supplier base, their complex inter-relationships of supply chain and channel partners, and the economic business conditions governing that industry. Not all the recommendations translate readily to industry in general.

Standardized Supplier Diversity Performance Metrics
The sub-committee favored the establishment of consistent definitions and measures for supplier diversity performance as a basic element of good management practice. Measuring successful adoption, of even the Five Key Recommendations,

demands some minimum definitions and standards across companies and across industries. Compulsory, complex and/or WBE-specific metrics have the potential to create undue bureaucracy for corporations and may not achieve the desired results. The Committee does recommend, however, some minor modifications to the previously published WBENC Balanced Scorecard that would provide an appropriate mechanism for measurement.

In Conclusion

Over the course of this book we have talked about light bulbs, building blocks, marriage and more. All of these things are important and helpful, but, at the end of the day, the bottom line in business is, almost always, "the bottom line." After all is said and done, the successful supplier, GME or not, will be the one who understands that his or her company must bring value to clients by delivering quality at a competitive price. In today's competitive environment, the tools for providing that quality include technology utilization, an eye toward globalization, having and maintaining the right credentials (including certification) and, most of all, identifying appropriate partners throughout the life cycle of one's business. That is the key to breaking into and remaining a valued part of the supply chain of America's top corporations.

While reading the stories, tips and advice in this book, you may have considered launching a new joint venture, forming a formal partnership, acquiring a company, developing a strategic alliance or creating another type of business relationship. Or, you may have developed a greater appreciation of your vendors, employees, bankers, family members and others as true partners in your business. There are countless definitions of "partner" and countless ways to make partnership work (or to make partnership end, if necessary). The diverse partnership stories in this book are only the tip of the iceberg, and I look forward to hearing about more successful GME partnerships in the future—how they begin, how they grow and how they confront challenges.

As you move forward with your own partnerships, I urge you to keep in mind the five building blocks that have appeared throughout the book—timing, financial resources, human capital, support networks and strategic vision—and to stay true to the "win-win-win" mentality of serving the needs of yourself, your partner and your valued clients and customers. With these crucial elements in place, you will be ahead of the pack when it comes to winning and keeping the contracts you desire. Partnership in all its forms is essential to your success and the success of GMEs as a thriving component of the U.S. economy.

Thank you for your partnership in support of this book and of WBENC. May all your partnerships be profitable!

Appendix A

WBENC Balanced Score Card

Women's Business Enterprise National Council
Balanced Score Card for WBE Program Process Improvement

WOMEN'S BUSINESS ENTERPRISE NATIONAL COUNCIL

Strategic Initiatives

Strategic Objective		Measure	Maximum Score	Company Score
Strengthen the Supply Chain	A	WBE Supplier Participation	25	
	B	Manages WBE Supplier Relationships	25	
	C	WBE Program Sustainability (see following page)	35	
Grow Revenue	D	Tracks revenue from WBE/Women Consumer Market(s) AND/OR corporate/government accounts	15	
		Total	**100**	

2002 Total WBE Spend	$		
# of 2002 Active WBE Suppliers			
Top WBE Supplier Spend as % of Total Base Spend	%		
		Maximum Score	**Company Score**
% WBE Spend to Total Spend	%	25	

	Maximum Score	**Company Score**
Tracks WBE Supplier Performance Metrics	10	
Tracks WBE Cost Savings	5	
Facilitates Growth of Targeted WBE Suppliers	10	

SB Services Inc.
bridging boundaries

Developed by SB Services, Inc. for WBENC.

Women's Business Enterprise National Council
Balanced Score Card for WBE Program Process Improvement

WOMEN'S BUSINESS ENTERPRISE NATIONAL COUNCIL

Strategic Objective	Measure	Maximum Score	Company Score	
Strengthen the Supply Chain	WBE Program Sustainability			**CEO Commitment**
		1		Corporate Policy Statement promoting the use of WBEs
		1		Active CEO leadership and involvement within the corporation
		1		Corporate WBE Goal
		1		Goals by Department or Commodity
		1		Cross Functional Leadership Team or Advisory Council
				Accountability for WBE Goals At All Levels
				WBE Program Performance linked to performance reviews and/or compensation for:
		1		Some Buyers
		1		All Buyers (If all buyers are included, score 2 points—1 above and 1 here)
		1		Senior Purchasing Management
		1		Cross Functional Management (i.e., internal customers outside of procurement)
		1		CEO/President
				Program Structure
		1		Full time employee to drive the initiative
		1		Requires 3rd party certification
		1		Requires 3rd party certification that includes a site visit (i.e., WBENC)
		13		Sub-Total This Page

SB Services Inc. bridging boundaries

Developed by SB Services, Inc. for WBENC.

Page

Women's Business Enterprise National Council
Balanced Score Card for WBE Program Process Improvement

WOMEN'S BUSINESS ENTERPRISE NATIONAL COUNCIL

Strategic Objective	Measure
Strengthen the Supply Chain	WBE Program Sustainability

Maximum Score	Company Score	
		Program Structure Continued
		Training has been conducted:
1		Within Purchasing/Supply Chain Management
1		Cross-Functionally to Key Stakeholders
1		Generate monthly/quarterly reports to track WBE spend; reports distributed to:
1		Buyers
1		Senior Purchasing Management
1		Cross Functional Stakeholders
1		President/CEO
1		Maintains corporate Supplier Diversity intranet website
		Proactively Managing the Supply Chain: Integrated WBEs into the following areas:
1		Into strategic sourcing
1		Into core commodity/service areas
1		Into marketing/advertising
1		Into accounting, legal, and/or /financial services
12		Sub-Total This Page

SB Services Inc.
bridging boundaries

Developed by SB Services, Inc. for WBENC.

Page -

Women's Business Enterprise National Council
Balanced Score Card for WBE Program Process Improvement

WOMEN'S BUSINESS ENTERPRISE NATIONAL COUNCIL

Strategic Objective	Measure
Strengthen the Supply Chain	WBE Program Sustainability

Maximum Score	Company Score	
		Proactively Managing the Supply Chain cont'd.
1		Spending with WBEs increased over the last 12 months (or last fiscal year)
1		Volume with the largest WBE exceeds .5% of Total Base Spend
1		Maintains internal directory of active WBE suppliers
1		Second Tier Process with required participation
1		Incentive for meeting objective and/or penalty for non-performance
		WBE Outreach
1		Facilitates WBE registration on corporate internet website
1		Conducts in-house vendor fairs to introduce WBEs to buyers
1		Participates in national/regional WBE trade fairs
1		Sources WBEs through industry trade groups/organizations
1		Maintains internal directory of potential WBE Suppliers
10		Sub-Total This Page

35		**Total Score for WBE Program Sustainability**

SB Services Inc. bridging boundaries

Developed by SB Services, Inc. for WBENC.

Page

Women's Business Enterprise National Council
Balanced Score Card for WBE Program Process Improvement

WOMEN'S BUSINESS ENTERPRISE NATIONAL COUNCIL

Instructions

Section A – WBE Supplier Participation: Complete the blue box first. Use 6% as the "desired state" for WBE participation and prorate 25 points accordingly. For example, if your corporation achieved 6% or more WBE participation, your score is 25 in Section A; if your corporation achieved 5% WBE participation, your score is 21 (5% divided by 6% = .83; .83*25 points = 21 points). Note, the goal is to minimize the amount of spend excluded from the base. In general, it is common to omit the following types of spend: employee reimbursements, taxes, royalties. Additional exclusions (like insurance, employee benefits, utilities, rent, etc.). should be minimized and carefully evaluated on a case-by-case basis *to ensure there is absolutely no opportunity* for considering women owned suppliers for that particular category. Remember, once a category is defined as an "excludable", you have, in effect, closed the door to potential consideration for any woman owned business in the future.

Section B – Manages WBE Supplier Relationships: This section refers to the extent to which the company proactively manages its relationships with women owned businesses. For example, corporations generally measure the performance of their largest suppliers. *The objective here is for at least some of your WBEs to be included in this process to document their added value as suppliers.* Complete the blue box first, add the total points for your company, and insert into "Company Score" for Section B. For example, if your corporation formally tracks the supplier performance of women owned businesses in your supply chain, ten points are awarded; if cost savings is included in the process, another five points are awarded. If your company proactively facilitates the growth of targeted WBE suppliers, another 10 points awarded for a total of 25 points in Section B.

Section C – WBE Program Sustainability: This section is detailed on pages two through four of the score card and refers to how the process is structured and positioned within your organization, including strategies employed to drive performance. Complete pages two to four by scoring points for the various activities your company has engaged in. Add the total number of points from pages two through four and insert in Section C on page one of the Score Card.

Section D - Links to Revenue: This section refers to the extent your corporation has leveraged integrating WBEs into the supply chain to generate sales/revenue. Documenting supplier diversity's impact on market share: 1) increases internal buy-in, 2) promotes innovative approaches to integrating and building the capacity of women owned businesses, 3) drives additional resources to continue integrating WBEs into the supply chain, and 4) builds brand equity with targeted customers to sustain and/or increase market share.

If your company sells to the government and/or other corporations that require women business development, and your company tracks this revenue, insert "15" into your company score. Or, if your company provides products/services sold to individual consumers, and your company tracks the amount of sales/revenue generated from women as consumers, insert "15" npany score.

SB Services Inc.
bridging boundaries

Developed by SB Services, Inc. for WBENC.

Page

Appendix B

The Zenith Group

Here is more detailed information, including membership criteria, for the Zenith Group, mentioned throughout *Partnering for Profit*:

The Zenith Group is a new and exciting program for those women owned businesses with revenues of $50 million and above. The Zenith Group brings together WPO and WBENC peers from across the country to drive business breakthroughs. The group meets twice during the year, once on the East Coast and once on the West Coast. This special group is being launched to achieve the following two objectives:

1. To provide cutting-edge information and strategies for successful and fast-growth companies.
2. To provide high-level business meetings and business development opportunities with Fortune 1000 companies.

Designed for certified entrepreneurial women, the WPO and WBENC will bring together highly motivated, highly successful women in a dynamic forum where they can harness the momentum of their successes and aim for bigger profits and bigger dreams. The synergy of the peer advisory group empowers members to achieve increased business and financial success as well as individual growth. As a result, each member exceeds performance expectations for her business and develops a more balanced personal life.

To be eligible, you must be a WPO member-at-large or chapter member (or join as a member) and WBENC-certified or eligible for certification (and will become certified within 120 days of joining the group). Participation is restricted to these larger sized businesses that share similar issues.

The typical meeting format begins with a group dinner Thursday evening, followed by a full-day session on Friday with a theme or topic chosen by the members and closes with a half-day session on Saturday. There might be a visiting expert in a particular field, and there is *always* intensive and powerful interaction within this exceptional group of peers. Relationships are strengthened and powerful new bonds are created. In addition to the roundtable experience, where mutually important issues are examined, the Zenith Group will provide scheduled meetings to meet suppliers from the Fortune 1000. Business development meetings will be arranged with these leading corporations to promote new opportunities.

For more information, please visit the Women Presidents' Organization at *www.womenpresidentsorg.com* or email *certification@womenpresidentsorg.com.*

Appendix C

Organizations

WBENC Women's Business Organization Partners

WBENC has 14 Partner Organizations across the country that handle certification for all 50 states and provide support and resources to WBEs on a local level.

Women's Business Enterprise Council-West
2266 S. Dobson Road, Suite 200
Mesa, AZ 85202
Phone: 480-775-5162
Fax: 480-775-5164
Web: *www.wbec-west.org*

Astra Women's Business Alliance
5 Centerpointe Drive, Suite 400
Lake Oswego, OR 97035
Phone: (971) 204-0220
Fax: (971) 204-0221
Web: *www.astrawba.org*

Center for Women & Enterprise
24 School Street, 7th Floor
Boston, MA 02108
Phone: (617) 536-0700
Fax: (617) 536-7373
Web: *www.cweonline.org*

Georgia Women's Business Council
231 Peachtree Street, NE
Atlanta, GA 30303
Phone: (678) 904-8470
Fax: (678) 904-8474
Web: *www.gwbc.biz*

Women's Business Enterprise Alliance
1900 North Loop West, Suite 270
Houston, TX 77018-8100
Phone: (713) 681-9232
Fax: (713) 681-9242
Web: *www.wbea-texas.org*

Michigan Women's Business Council
2002 Hogback Road, Suite 12
Ann Arbor, MI 48105
Phone: (734) 677-1400
Fax: (734) 677-1465

Women's Business Enterprise Council-Southeast
100 E. Broad St., Suite 2460
Columbus, Ohio 43215
Phone: (614) 228-4150
Toll Free: 1-866-WBE-CERT
Fax: (614) 228-4160

Women Presidents' Educational Organization - New York
155 E. 55th, Suite 4H
New York, NY 10022
Phone: (212) 688-4114
Fax: (212) 688-4766
Web: *www.womenpresidentsorg.com*

Women Presidents' Educational Organization - DC
1120 Connecticut Avenue, NW
Suite 1000
Washington, DC 20036
Phone: (202) 872-1642
Fax: (202) 872-5505
Web: *www.womenpresidentsorg.com*

Women's Business Council Gulf Coast
400 Poydras, Ste. 1730
New Orleans, LA 70130
Phone: (504) 680-1886
Fax: (504) 680-6412
Web: *www.wbcGulfCoast.org*

Women's Business Council - Southwest
2201 N. Collins, Suite 158
Arlington, TX 76011
Phone: (817) 299-0566
Fax: (817) 299-0949
Web: *www.wbcsouthwest.org*

Women's Business Development Center/Chicago
8 South Michigan, Suite 400
Chicago, IL 60603
Phone: (312) 853-3477 ext. 20
Fax: (312) 853-0145
Web: *www.wbdc.org*

Women's Business Development Center/Miami
11205 S. Dixie Highway, Suite 104
Miami, FL 33156
Phone: (305) 971-9473
Fax: (305) 971-7061

Women's Business Development Center/Philadelphia
1315 Walnut Street, Suite 1116
Philadelphia, PA 19107-4711
Phone: (215) 790-9232
Fax: (215) 790-9231
Web: *www.womensbdc.org*

Federal OSDBU Offices

Defense Contract Management Agency (DCMA)
6350 Walker Lane
Alexandria, VA 22310
Phone: (703) 428-0786
Fax: (703) 428-3578

Defense Information Systems Agency (DISA)
701 S. Courthouse Road, D04 Room 1108B
Arlington, VA 22204-2199
Phone: (703) 607-6436
Fax: (703) 607-4173

Defense Logistics Agency (DLA)
8725 John J. Kingman Road, DB Room 1127
Ft. Belvoir, VA 22060-6221
Phone: (703) 767-1652
Fax: (703) 767-1670

Department of the Air Force
The Pentagon, SASSB 1060 Air Force
Washington, DC 20330-1060
Phone: (703) 696-1103
Fax: (703) 696-1170

Department of the Army
The Pentagon, Room 3B514
Washington, DC 20310-0106
Phone: (703) 697-2868
Fax: (703) 693-3898

Department of Defense
1777 North Kent Street, Suite 9100
Washington, DC 22209
Phone: (703) 588-8620
Fax: (703) 588-7561

Department of the Navy
720 Kennon St., N.E.
Washington Navy Yard, DC 20374-5015
Phone: (202) 685-6485
Fax: (202) 685-6865

Federal Deposit Insurance Corporation
801 17th St., NW, Room 1250
Washington, DC 20434
Phone: (202) 416-2457
Fax: (202) 416-2466

National Aeronautics and Space Administration
300 E Street, SW, Room 9K70, Code K
Washington, DC 20546
Phone: (202) 358-2088
Fax: (202) 358-3261

National Science Foundation
4201 Wilson Boulevard, Room 527
Arlington, VA, 22230
Phone: (703) 292-7082
Fax: (703) 292-9055

Nuclear Regulatory Commission
Office of Small Business and Civil Rights
11545 Rockville Pike, MS T2 F18
Rockville, MD 20852
Phone: (301) 415-7380
Fax: (301) 415-5953

Smithsonian Institution
Office of Equal Employment and Minority Affairs
750 9th Street, Suite 8100 MRC 921
Washington, DC 20560-0921
Phone: (202) 275-0157
Fax (202) 275-2055

Social Security Adminstration
Office of Acquisition and Grants
G-C-7 East High Rise Building
6401 Security Boulevard
Baltimore, Maryland 21235
Phone: (410) 965-7467
Fax: (410) 597-1548

Transportation Security Administration
TSA HQ-West Building, 4th Floor, TSA-14
601 S. 12th Street
Arlington, VA 22202
Phone: (571) 227-2070

U.S. Agency for International Development
Ronald Reagan Building, USAID/OSDBU/MRC
1300 Pennsylvania Ave., NW, Room 7.8E
Washington, DC 20523-7800
Phone: (202) 712-1500
Fax: (202) 216-3056

U.S. Department of Agriculture
14th & Independence Avenue, SW, 1566 South Building
Washington, DC 20250-9501
Phone: (202) 720-7117
Fax: (202) 720-3001

U.S. Department of Commerce
14th & Constitution Avenue, NW, Room H-6411
Washington, DC 20230
Phone: (202) 482-1472
Fax: (202) 482-0501

U.S. Department of Education
400 Maryland Ave., S.W.
Room 7048, PCP
Washington, D.C. 20202-0521
Phone: (202) 245-6300
Fax: (202) 245-6304

U.S. Department of Energy
1000 Independence Avenue, S.W.
Room # 5B-148
Washington, DC 20585
Phone: (202) 586-7377
Fax: (202) 586-5488

U.S. Department of Health and Human Services
200 Independence Avenue, SW, Room 360-G
Washington, DC 20201
Phone: (202) 690-6670
Fax: (202) 260-4872

U.S. Department of Housing and Urban Development
451 7th Street, SW, Room 3130
Washington, DC 20410-1000
Phone: (202) 708-1428
Fax: (202) 708-7642

U.S. Department of Justice
1331 Pennsylvania Avenue, NW
National Place Building, Room 1010
Washington, DC 20530
Phone: (202) 616-0521
Fax: (202) 616-1717

U.S. Department of Labor
200 Constitution Avenue, NW, Room C-2318
Washington, DC 20210
Director: Jose Lira
Phone: (202) 693-6460
Fax: (202) 693-6485

U.S. Department of State
SA-6, Room L500
Washington, DC 20522
Phone: (703) 875-6822
Fax: (703) 875-6825

U.S. Department of Transportation
400 7th Street, SW, Room 9414
Washington, DC 20590
Phone: (202) 366-1930
Fax: (202) 366-7228

U.S. Department of the Treasury
1500 Pennsylvania Ave., NW, Mail Code: 655 15th/6099
Washington, DC 20220
Phone: (202) 622-0793
Fax: (202) 622-4963

U.S. Department of Homeland Security
Attn: OSDBU/Room 3514
Washington, DC 20528
Phone: (202) 692-4343
Fax: (202) 777-8467

U.S. Department of the Interior
1849 C Street, NW, MS2252
Washington, D.C. 20240
Phone: (202) 208-3493
Fax: (202) 208-7444

U.S. Environmental Protection Agency
1200 Pennsylvania Avenue, NW, Code 1230-A
Washington, DC 20460
Phone: (202) 564-4100
Fax: (202) 501-0756

U.S. Postal Service
475 L'Enfant Plaza SW Room 4430
Washington, DC 20260-6204
Phone: (202) 268-4633
Fax: (202) 268-4012

U.S. Department of Veterans Affairs
810 Vermont Avenue, NW (Mail Stop 00SB)
Washington, DC 20420-0001
Phone: (202) 565-8124, toll-free (800) 949-8387

Fax: (202) 565-8156
U.S. General Services Administration
1800 F Street, NW
Washington, DC 20405
Phone: (202) 501-1021
Fax: (202) 208-5938

Other Organizations and Resources for GMEs

Here are some useful web sites for more information on the organizations and topics covered in *Partnering for Profit.* Please note that WBENC assumes no responsibility for, nor does it endorse, the information contained in any of the web sites mentioned.

Associations, Networking Groups and Organizations

American Subcontractors Association (ASA)
www.ASAonline.com

Association for Conflict Resolution
www.acresolution.org

Center for Women's Business Research
www.womensbusinessresearch.org

Institute for Supply Management
www.ism.ws

Institute for Women's Leadership
www.womensleadership.com

International Franchise Association
www.franchise.org

Latin Business Association (LBA)
www.lbausa.com

National Association of Small Disadvantaged Businesses (NASDB)
www.nasdb.org

National Association of Women Business Owners (NAWBO)
www.nawbo.org

National Association of Women in Construction
www.nawic.org

National Black Chamber of Commerce
www.nationalbcc.org

National Center for American Indian Enterprise Development (NCAIED)
www.ncaied.org

National Indian Business Association
www.nibanetwork.org

National Minority Supplier Development Council (NMSDC)
www.nmsdcus.org

National Women's Business Council (NWBC)
www.nwbc.gov

Native American Business Alliance
www.native-american-bus.org

Online Women's Business Center
www.onlinewbc.gov

Quantum Leaps, Inc.
www.quantumleapsinc.org

U.S. Chamber of Commerce
www.uschamber.org

U.S. Hispanic Chamber of Commerce
www.ushcc.com

U.S. Pan Asian American Chamber of Commerce
www.uspaacc.com

The Veterans Corporation
www.veteranscorp.org

Women's Business Enterprise National Council (WBENC)
www.wbenc.org

Women Construction Owners & Executives, USA (WCOE)
www.wcoeusa.org

Women Impacting Public Policy (WIPP)
www.wipp.org

Women in Technology International (WITI)
www.witi.com

Women Presidents' Organization (WPO)
www.womenpresidentsorg.com

World Wide Minority Business Network
www.mbnet.com

Government

Central Contractor Registration
www.ccr.gov

Department of Defense Mentor-Protégé Program
http://www.acq.osd.mil/sadbu/mentor_protege/

Fed Biz Opps: Federal Business Opportunities
www.fedbizopps.gov

Federal Access
www.fedaccess.com

Minority Business Development Agency (MBDA)
www.mbda.gov

SUB-*Net:* U.S. Small Business Administration Subcontracting Network
http://web.sba.gov/subnet

The Federal Marketplace
www.fedmarket.com

U.S. Small Business Administration
www.sba.gov

WomenBiz
www.womenbiz.gov

Women's Entrepreneurship in the 21st Century
www.Women-21.gov

GME and Small Business Publications & Web Sites

American Indian Report
www.americanindianreport.com

Asian Enterprise
www.asianenterprise.com

Black Enterprise
www.blackenterprise.com

Diversity Inc.
www.diversityinc.com

Diversity Information Resources
www.diversityinforesources.com

DiversityBusiness
www.diversitybusiness.com

Enterprising Women Magazine
www.enterprisingwomen.com

Entreworld
www.entreworld.org

Hispanic Business
www.hispanicbusiness.com

Latina Style
www.latinastyle.com

MBE (Minority Business Entrepreneur) Magazine
www.mbemag.com

Minority Business News USA
www.minoritybusinessnews.com

Small Business Television
www.sbtv.com

WE: Women's Enterprise
www.womens-enterprise.com

Appendix D

GME Companies Mentioned in Partnering for Profit

The following WBEs and MBEs mentioned in *Partnering for Profit* submitted information about their companies. They are listed in order of their appearance in the book.

Chapter One

Julie White
McKinley Marketing Partners
www.mckinleyinc.com

Julie White is an independent contractor who has 20+ years of advertising and marketing management experience. She works with corporations, not-for-profit organizations and government agencies, as well as McKinley Marketing Partners, in a variety of industry categories. She especially provides support in branding and corporate identity, business-to-business and consumer advertising, market research and strategic communications planning and analysis.

McKinley Marketing Partners, Inc. was founded in 1995 as a pioneer provider of Interim Marketing Managerssm (IMMs®) to Fortune 1000 companies, trade associations, and start-up companies. Woman-owned/operated, McKinley Marketing Partners, Inc. is based in Alexandria, Virginia (just outside Washington, DC). They have offices in Virginia and Texas, and resources available in most major metropolitan areas. McKinley provides IMMs® to help its clients meet their immediate, project-based marketing needs.

Marilyn Carlson Nelson
Carlson Companies
www.carlson.com

Carlson Companies is a global leader in the marketing, travel, and hospitality industries. Among the names in the Carlson family of brands and services are: Regent® International Hotels; Radisson® Hotels & Resorts; Park Plaza® Hotels & Resorts; Country Inns & Suites By Carlson®; Park Inn® hotels; Radisson Seven Seas Cruises®; T.G.I. Friday's® and Pick Up Stix® restaurants; Carlson Wagonlit Travel®; Cruise Holidays®; Results Travel®; Carlson Destination Marketing Services®; Carlson Leisure Travel Services®; SeaMaster Cruises®; SinglesCruise.com®; CW Government Travel®; Carlson Marketing Group®, the world leader in Relationship Marketing; Peppers & Rogers Group®; and Gold Points Reward Network®, an online/offline consumer loyalty program.

Ranked among the largest privately held corporations in the United States, Carlson Companies is based in Minneapolis, Minnesota. Carlson-related brands and services employ about 190,000 people in more than 140 countries. Carlson Companies is on Working Mother magazine's 2001-2004 list of "The 100 Best Companies for Working Mothers" and Fortune magazine's 2002 list of "The 100 Best Companies to Work For."

Nancy Michaels
Grow Your Business Network
www.growyourbusinessnetwork.com

Grow Your Business Network works with minority and woman business owners who want to grow their small businesses on a budget. Most small business owners are great at what they do, but struggle with how to maintain a marketing plan that helps to grow their businesses. Growing one's customer base can be fun, positive and exciting if tackled it the right way. Grow Your Business Network provides laser coaching, intensive tele-classes, manuals, workbooks, and educational resources for small business owners who want to cultivate new business and make more money.

Grow Your Business Network also works with large corporations that want to reach the small business marketplace in a meaningful way, to increase their loyal customer base. They do this through web cast program management, in-store seminars, national speaking tours, conference planning, sponsorship opportunities and consulting.

Chapter Two

Lynne Marie Finn
Superior Staffing Services, Inc.
www.superiorstaffingservices.com

Superior Staffing Services, Inc., a WBENC-certified full service staffing solutions company, is one of the few national staffing companies that is woman-owned and operated. Headquartered in Williamsville, New York, Superior Staffing has offices throughout the U.S. and has recently expanded its operations into Canada. Superior provides temporary staffing, direct placement services, managed staffing programs and outsourced HR solutions primarily to Fortune 500 companies.

Superior's customers span a wide range of industries, including automotive, aircraft/aerospace, banking, call centers, defense, electronics, entertainment, insurance, manufacturing, semiconductor, software, telecommunications, transportation and utilities.

Superior Staffing was one of the frontrunners in developing web-automated labor management tools, and its proprietary Labor Activity Management System ($LAMS^{360}$) is now in its fifth generation. $LAMS^{360}$ is utilized in outsourced managed staffing programs to automate many processes in the acquisition of temporary labor resulting in significant cost savings, reduced cycle time and improved candidate quality.

Charline Guidry
Diamond Oil Field Supply
www.dofs.net

Diamond Oil Field Supply services the marine, industrial and oilfield business community. They sell to major and independent oil & gas companies, offshore operators, ship builders, barge repair companies, fabrication, offshore/onshore construction companies and also to the many companies who service them. Diamond buys direct from the manufacturer, distributor or local supplier and can supply all typical products needed for new construction, maintenance and refurbishment projects, as well as all supplies for daily living on the offshore platform.

They are considered "one-stop shopping" to the offshore platform and can receive one order which may include ball valves, grating, chemical pumps, gauges, safety equipment, tools, microwave, washer, dryer, office supplies, computer equipment, paint, linen, pots and pans. Diamond can sell any type of valve, pipe, fittings, steel and all fasteners to ship builders, barge repair, fabrication and construction companies.

Roz Alford & Nancy Williams
ASAP Staffing
www.asapstaffingllc.com

The company's mission is to provide quality service and expertise to its clients and consultants while delivering excellence to meet the needs of the industry. ASAP Staffing, (ASAP) is a privately held, woman-owned corporation that has enjoyed strong, steady growth since December, 1989. ASAP Staffing was launched as a direct market response to the need for highly skilled information technology consultants. The initial goal of ASAP was to provide quality resources to the business community. ASAP provides highly trained and experienced staff in specific technologies to Fortune 500 firms. ASAP provides all levels of consulting including lan/wan/pc help desk support and administration, application development and maintenance, database design and project management. Partnerships with client companies have been the key to the company's success and growth. Regardless of the size or length of the project, ASAP utilizes an extensive database to provide client companies with the necessary support they need. This network of consultants enables ASAP to respond quickly to the needs of its clients with the right technical resources the first time.

Chapter Three

Judith Ritter
Ritter Contracting
www.rittercontracting.com

Ritter Contracting, Inc. specializes in the union construction market for commercial, public works, airports, health care and highway projects. Ritter Contracting employs skilled union personnel and supplies a wide range of competitively priced construction materials and equipment. The company is dedicated to solving its clients' construction problems with ongoing service and follow-up. Ritter Contracting becomes part of "the team" and produces a quality product that comes in on budget and on time.

Denise Stovell
Stovell Marketing & Public Relations
www.stovellmarketingpr.com

Stovell Marketing & Public Relations (SMPR) knows how to learn about your company, and listen to your needs, helping to ensure the creation of winning marketing communications programs. SMPR also understands that effective marketing and public relations centers on identifying strategies that keep your bottom line on the top line.

SMPR is a full-service marketing and pubic relations firm,

specializing in marketing strategy, public relations, content development and event management. The company has extensive experience developing programs for corporate America, women and minority business owners and nonprofit organizations.

Rebecca Boenigk
Neutral Posture
www.iGoErgo.com

Neutral Posture was founded in 1989 when the mother/daughter team of Jaye Congleton and Rebecca Congleton Boenigk recognized an opportunity to manufacture and distribute the Neutral Posture® chair—a seating system of pressure-reducing contours and custom-fitting adjustments. Supporting the neutral body posture discovered by NASA, the Neutral Posture seating system was designed to accommodate everybody, small to tall, with over 10 standard adjustments.

As the only certified Women's Business Enterprise in seating, Neutral Posture has rewritten the rules of quality, customer service and value with the most exceptional product offering in the furniture industry. Through a nationwide dealer and sales representative network, Neutral Posture delivers ergonomic seating solutions to employees everywhere, helping to make offices safer, healthier and productive. Neutral Posture focuses on continuous quality improvement and product innovation, through market-driven research and the changing needs of workers everywhere. From ergonomic niche products to state-of-the-art mid-market products, Neutral Posture is the new corporate seating standard for ergonomic-conscious employers and organizations throughout North America.

Julia Hubbel
The Hubbel Group
www.principlednetworking.com

Julia Hubbel is a successful entrepreneur, speaker, author and prize-winning journalist who specializes in teaching people how to build lasting, mutually-beneficial relationships. She is an expert on the art of Principled Networking©, a system she designed based on her experiences in building a highly successful professional women's network in the Pacific Northwest, The Hubbel Group. Julia provides speeches, training, consulting, keynotes and customized programs in business relationships that reduce turnover and enhance profitability in Fortune 500 companies and membership organizations.

Julia's story is profiled in the bestselling book *Networking Magic,* by *Guerilla Marketing* authors Rick Frishman and Jill Lublin. Her high energy, interactive style has made her a popular speaker at conferences and a valued profitability partner for organizations where business relationships could be improved.

Ralph G. Moore
Ralph G. Moore & Associates (RGMA)
www.rgma.com

For two decades, RGMA has provided comprehensive consulting services to hundreds of small businesses and organizations. To compete effectively in this re-engineered economy, emerging businesses need a variety of consulting services to compliment internal resources. RGMA provides growing businesses with the expertise and counsel necessary to achieve controlled business growth. RGMA's business advisory consulting services includes: organizational assessments, strategic planning, business planning, financial analysis, capital acquisition, marketing plans, certification, mentor-protégé program development, board of directors development, disparity/fact-finding studies and affirmative action plans.

Cathy Dougherty
Dougherty Sprague Environmental
www.dsei.com

Dougherty Sprague Environmental (DSE) is a seven-year-old environmental engineering and consulting company based near Dallas, Texas. DSE specializes in soil and groundwater assessments and remediation for private, municipal and government clients. The company also does emergency response and Superfund work for the Environmental Protection Agency (EPA). DSE has been a contractor for START since 2002 and participated in the Columbia Shuttle Recovery and response for the Florida hurricanes in Fall of 2004. DSE is an 8(a), woman-owned company and also a licensed UST contractor, asbestos and lead firm. DSE currently has an environmental GSA schedule contract, GS10-0616P, SIN1-4 and 8.

Clarice Kennedy
CCN
www.ccncorp.com

CCN, Inc. is a privately held, certified Woman Business Enterprise. Founded in 1989 by Chairman and CEO, Clarice Kennedy, CCN provides information technology service management solutions.

For the past 16 years, CCN has been offering services to the Fortune 500 community across multiple industry verticals with specific strengths in Help Desk support. CCN's industry best practice approach is based around the Information Technology Infrastructure Library (ITIL) and IT Service Management (ITSM) framework. This approach allows the company to assist its clients in creating and maintaining world-class support and IT environments.

CCN's focus is fostering effective and efficient IT and support center organizations. CCN researches, maintains and implements the highest industry standards within its Customer Care Solutions practice.

Carmen Castillo
Superior Design International (SDI)
www.sdintl.com

SDI is a leader in strategic outsourcing—from enterprise level supply chain management programs to global technical and professional recruitment initiatives. SDI is committed to providing world class programs while producing documented cost savings. From the two cornerstones of world class quality (SDI is ISO 9001:2000 certified) and cost effective services, the company has built multinational programs that adapt to changing market conditions, grow with the needs of its clients and produce real value.

Pamela O'Rourke
ICON Information Systems
www.iconconsultants.com

Icon Information Consultants, LP is a Houston-based, woman-owned company that specializes in identifying and recruiting highly qualified information technology, engineering, accounting and finance professionals at all levels and skills. Since 1997, Icon has grown from a start-up operation to a premier staffing organization. The company's services include consulting, staff augmentation, project management and payroll. Icon Information Consultants, LP has gained its superior reputation by being customer service driven, responsive, thorough and ethical. The company culture sets a new standard for customer service and its clients are responding to the positive business practices. As a result, Icon has reached a "top tier" or preferred vendor status.

Nancy Connolly
Smart Page Technologies and Lasertone Corporation
www.lasertone.com
www.smartpagetech.com

Founded in 1989, Lasertone Corporation is the nation's leading woman-owned provider of network printer hardware, software, services and supplies, earning over $12.7 million in revenue in 2004. Located in Littleton, Massachusetts, Lasertone employs over 30 people, administers an extensive cartridge-recycling program, and distributes approximately 65,000 Lasertone-brand and OEM cartridges annually.

Launched on November 1, 2004, Smart Page Technologies (Lasertone's affiliate) delivers outsourced print management services through an integration of hardware and software solutions, providing companies the ability to increase efficiencies and reduce the costs of their document environments. The company employs a dedicated team of sales and service professionals and realized over $1 million in revenue in 2004. Smart Page Technologies is headquartered in Littleton, Massachusetts, with a sales and demonstration office in Boston.

Lasertone Corporation and Smart Page Technologies' workplaces reflect a diverse environment. Forty-one percent of Lasertone's employees and 57 percent of Smart Page Technologies' employees are either women or minorities. Lasertone is certified by WBENC and also by the State Office of Minority- and Woman-Owned Business Assistance of Massachusetts. Through its integrated supplier diversity program, Lasertone maintained a 10 percent diversity spend in 2004, representing over $1 million spent with MWBE suppliers.

Debbie Faraone
The Elements
www.the-elementsinc.com

The Elements, a WBENC-certified, woman-owned business, provides creative and innovative product solutions. The company's clients look to the firm for fresh, innovative ideas to reinforce and promote their company message and brand. In addition to being an ad specialty distributor, The Elements represents a variety of unique artists and distinguished retail lines, and design and manufacture its own custom line of business accessories and writing instruments. The company's creative custom capabilities and marketing insight sets The Elements apart from typical ad specialty companies.

Barbara Vinar
Cable Connection & Supply

Cable Connection & Supply provides cable TV systems; data systems, including LAN equipment; fiber and cable, including cables/cable assemblies, connectors and splicing/termination equipment; passive components; telecom terminal equipment; and test and measurement equipment.

Himanshu Bhatia
Rose International
www.roseint.com

Himanshu and Gulab Bhatia founded Rose International in 1993. In 1995, St. Louis-based Rose committed to becoming a world-class IT provider, and a period of rapid growth ensued that continues to this day. This growth is a result of building solid partnerships with its clients to provide high quality service at a reasonable price, along with the company's ability to retain top-notch employees. Rose has a strong track record of repeat business from its clients, while continuing to win new clients on a consistent basis. The firm's leadership team has over

100 years of combined technology services experience with such companies as EDS, IBM, DEC, and Boeing. Rose has nearly 1,000 employees worldwide and numerous branch locations. The company also has an impressive client list, including ChevronTexaco, the Department of Defense, SBC, the State of Missouri and Toyota, among others.

Betsy Mordecai
MorSports & Events
www.morevents.com

MorEvents is full-service event management firm, specializing in sports hospitality, meeting management, conference planning, trade show management and special events management. For nearly two decades, members of the MorEvents staff have provided many of the world's finest corporations with top-notch hospitality, incentive travel and meeting coordination.

MorEvents has earned its success through a simplistic but creative approach to event and program management, the recruitment of exceptional individuals and adherence to the highest professional and ethical standards.

While creativity and imaginative solutions are at the heart of the company's delivery, MorSports has placed vast significance on a tangible, process-driven approach to project management. The company enjoys a partner relationship with many of its long-term clients, which reflects the added value that MorSports brings to the programs that it creates and executes.

Patricia Vanderpool
EAP Lifestyle Management
www.eaplifestyle.com

EAP Lifestyle Management, LLC is a company specializing in comprehensive employee assistance program services and work/life benefits on a local and national level. EAP Lifestyle

Management contracts with employers to help individuals deal with business and family pressures. Employers have a genuine concern for the well-being and betterment of their employees. When employees experience emotional, family, alcohol, drug, financial or legal problems, EAP Lifestyle Management provides early intervention for such issues. Assistance is also offered for childcare and eldercare referral, job loss, relocation and on-site services. When an employee or family member is helped, the company receives a dividend on its most important investment.

EAP Lifestyle Management provides top-quality employee assistance program services, including counseling services and workplace seminars and training, and work/life benefits, such as legal and financial assessment and referral. Programs are individually tailored to meet the needs of each company, with an extensive national database for providers and professionals nationwide. Access is available 24 hours a day, 7 days a week, and confidentiality is strictly respected for all referrals. EAP Lifestyle Management, LLC is CCR registered and qualified to bid on government contracts.

Carol Louis
Louis Companies
www.louiscompanies.com

Louis Companies is a manufacturer of fine lithographic and commercial printing.

The company is proficient in providing the graphic communications which your company requires to do business; Louis distributes to you through a network of manufacturers and services, who sell only to the trade. The company offers promotional product programs to provide incentive and safety awards, gifts and promotional advertising ideas, including wearables such as shirts and caps.

Louis Companies is large enough to handle the needs of a major corporation, yet small enough to be sure that each order is handled with the kind of uncompromising care that has set is apart from the rest of the industry. The company acts as the single source for all your printing, warehouse and distribution needs, and offers complete services in multiple product lines, such as business forms, commercial printing, labels, envelopes, specialty advertising and promotional products. Louis Companies takes pride in its ability to get the job done for its clients in the face of a complex and changing industry.

Jodi Clausman and Kelly Hess
Global Legal
Global Strategic Sourcing
www.globallegal.us
www.globalstrategicsourcing.com

Global Legal is an alliance of diversity-owned companies who specialize in large document and labor intensive cases from initial discovery through trial. Service offerings include legal staffing, legal copies, court reporting, record retrieval, document management, trial consulting and trial graphics. Global Legal provides a "one-stop shop" atmosphere with each alliance partner providing unsurpassed service in their area of expertise.

Julie Garella
McColl Garella
www.mccollgarella.com

Founded by Hugh McColl, the former chairman of Bank of America, and Julie Garella, McColl Garella is an investment banking firm that focuses on woman-owned and woman-run companies. It provides advice on buy-side and sell-side opportunities and raises private and strategic capital for its clients. The firm's focus includes: media and entertainment, technology, retail, healthcare, financial services, luxury and organic brands. McColl Garella is based in Charlotte, North Carolina.

Chapter Four

Janice Bryant Howroyd
ACT 1

The ACT 1 Group is a dynamic business focused on human capital management and technical, professional and administrative staffing. The company focuses on supporting best-practice business process, utilizing over 25 years of experience since its founding.

Jo Ann Brumit
KARLEE
www.karlee.com

KARLEE is a woman-owned provider of customized, integrated manufacturing services, such as sheet metal fabrication, precision machining, cabling, electromechanical assembly and process coating. KARLEE is diversified across several industry sectors, including medical, semi-conductor, telecommunications, nuclear, defense and commercial. To support business solutions, KARLEE offers a full range of services from e-business to total supply chain management, prototyping, and concurrent engineering. KARLEE has over 30 years of experience providing new product development engineering services for enclosures, component parts, box build and cabinets.

Ranjini Poddar
Artech Information Systems
www.artechinfo.com.

Artech Information Systems LLC is a preferred Tier-1 IT services provider to more than 20 Fortune 500 companies, providing IT consulting and staff augmentation, turnkey project management, infrastructure management, eCommerce and eBusiness and business process outsourcing. Since 1992, Artech's solutions have been designed to address all areas of critical needs in managing clients' strategic eBusiness and IT investments globally.

Artech has been recognized as an SBA Contractor of the Year; "Top Performer Quality, Cost and Timeliness" by Dun & Bradstreet; Department of Defense Mentor Protégé Nunn Perry Award winner; "Fast 25" by the Women Presidents' Organization and *Fast Company*; finalist, Ernst & Young Entrepreneur of the Year program; Top 50 Asian American in Business; and three times as a New Jersey Fast 50 Company by Deloitte & Touche.

Based in Morristown, New Jersey, Artech has regional offices in Fremont, California and McLean, Virginia, as well as a Level 4 SEI-CMM compliant and ISO 9001 certified offshore development facility in India and five field offices throughout the United States. Artech is a certified Minority and Women Owned Business Enterprise.

Ellie Halter
Schnipke Engraving Co.

The Schnipke Engraving Co. was founded in 1962 by Ellie Halter's parents, Leonard and Pauline Schnipke. The company remains under the ownership of the Schnipke family and became certified as a Women's Business Enterprise in July of 2002.

The company provides tool design and tool fabrication capabilities for its injection molding services. In addition to making new molds that meet the exacting requirements of its customers, this tooling capability provides Schnipke with the in-house ability to perform the mold maintenance and repair required in this type of molding. In 1983, Schnipke started specializing in very small, complex precision molded components for the medical and electronic industry. The company has established itself as an expert and reliable provider of highly complex surgical stapling cartridge assemblies and other precision components. Schnipke performs specialized assembly operations, which incorporate specialized fixturing designed and fabricated by Schnipke Engraving, vision system inspections and various types of automation.

Schnipke Engraving currently has two facilities—its original plant in Ottoville, Ohio and its newer plant in Tucson, Arizona, which opened in October of 2003.

Pamela C. Shafer
New Orleans Copper, Inc.
www.neworleanscopperinc.com

New Orleans Copper is a major pipe and tube bending company. It is a third generation owned and operated corporation which has been in business since the 1930s. The company services the oil and gas industry, the shipbuilding and marine service industry, the power plant industry and the construction industry, just to name a few. New Orleans Copper works with WBE major corporation sponsors, such as ChevronTexaco, Shell, ExxonMobil and Entergy. The company works with project managers and project engineers in providing pipe bends to complete their fabrication jobs. It can save welding by doing one-piece expansion loops, compound bends, offsets, spools and riser bends. New Orleans Copper also does structural bends with channel, I-beams and plate. The company has been a certified WBE with the Gulf Coast and Texas regions since 2003.

Beatriz (Betty) Manetta
Argent Technologies
www.argentassociates.com

Argent is a total end-to-end solutions provider and an MWBE, headquartered in New Jersey with facilities and capabilities nationwide. Argent offers complete supply chain management capabilities, including warehousing, distribution and fulfillment, product procurement, materials management and logistics, just-in-time inventory control, packaging and financing programs. Argent is also a network infrastructure services company consisting of core competencies that focus on network engineering and installation of transport, power, remote terminals and wireless products. Argent is a reseller/distributor for network and data products including Lucent, Nortel, Marconi, Tyco, Valere power and Cisco.

Lisa Hanlon
TelTech Communications
www.teltechcomm.com

TelTech Communications, LLC is a supplier of network infrastructure equipment and related services for wireless and wireline carriers and corporate IT departments. TelTech specializes in remanufactured equipment—OEM tested and certified, with OEM-backed warranty. TelTech has developed the expertise to supply bundled solutions, a mix of new and remanufactured equipment, providing the latest technology platforms with the cost savings of remanufactured components. Additionally, TelTech provides asset management and consignment sales, testing and repair, logistics and materials management, end-of-life (discontinued availability) services, network engineering, program management, field engineering and installation.

Olivia Fox Cabane
Spitfire Communications
www.spitfireteam.com

Spitfire Communications helps clients increase their business—and have fun doing it! Through Spitfire's consulting, training and private coaching, each client becomes a master business developer, networking with ease, grace and efficiency through the company's custom-tailored business development training programs.

Mary Cantando
WomanBusinessOwner.com
www.WomanBusinessOwner.com

WomanBusinessOwner.com is a national advisory, speaking and publishing firm, focusing on women who own multimillion dollar businesses.

The firm's president, Mary Cantando, is a recognized expert on growing woman-owned businesses, and is a featured speaker at national and international events. She serves as a media source for publications such as the Wall Street Journal, Enterprising Women, Fast Company, Selling Power and Entrepreneur magazine. And, she writes monthly columns for four entrepreneurial women's publications.

Cantando's twelve years as an entrepreneurial executive, coupled with four years of focused research on women business owners, positions her to provide unique growth insights for women entrepreneurs.

Cantando sits on the National Board of the Women Presidents' Organization. Her business is certified by WBENC and she serves on WBENC's National Women's Enterprise Leadership Forum. She serves on the Advisory Board of Enterprising Women magazine and is the Business Growth Advisor for Women Entrepreneurs, Inc.

Juanita "Nita" Burgoon
Burgoon Company
www.burgooncompany.com

The award-winning Burgoon Company was started by Nita Burgoon in 1988 with $1,000, which had been earmarked for a vacation. In 2005, Burgoon Company expects sales in excess of $25,000,000. This 8a/SDB/Hubzone/WBENC-certified small business is a wholesale distributor and strategic supply ally for a variety of companies, such as Grainger industrial supply, Fisher Scientific, VWR Scientific, Sigma Chemicals and many others.

Julia Klein
C.H. Briggs
www.chbriggs.com/corporate

C.H. Briggs is one of the largest independently-owned specialty building material distributors in the industry. In business for over 45 years, C.H. Briggs has forged a reputation for unparalleled service, strong customer relationships, and technology and e-business leadership. The company offers building materials and interior finishing products for commercial/retail space construction and facilities management. Products include: bathroom vanity tops (ADA-compliant), horizontal and vertical surfacing materials, countertop materials, hardware, sinks, lavatories, toilet partitions, laminate, melamine, particleboard, MDF, safety products, sandpaper and production supplies and ergonomic workspace accessories (i.e. keyboard trays, CPU holders). With over 160 employees, C.H. Briggs continues to grow and expansion has included the construction of a new 18,000 sq. ft. office building.

Chapter Five

Janice Pellar
EMCO Technologies
www.emcobr.com

EMCO provides sales, service and rentals of communications and information technologies, such as personal computers networks, two-way radios (Motorola) and emergency warning systems. EMCO also provides web site development and hosting.

Joyce Bosc
Boscobel Marketing Communications
www.boscobel.com

Boscobel Marketing Communications, Inc., is one of the Washington, DC-area's leading and most respected branding and PR firms. For over 25 years, Boscobel has provided integrated public relations, marketing, branding and advertising solutions for government and industry. Boscobel's brand is passionate, creative, fun and thorough, and the company works to drive your competition nuts with its enormous clip books. Founded by noted branding authority Joyce Bosc, the company's comprehensive and effective solutions are best known for the launch of America Online and the ITES RFP positioning of NCI Information Systems. Other client successes include Appian, ITS Corporation, Intelsat General Corporation, STG, Inc., the U.S. Coast Guard and the National Foundation for Credit Counseling (NFCC).

Nina Vaca
Pinnacle Technical Resources
www.pinnacle1.com

Pinnacle is a leading provider of solutions-based and managed information technology services as well as flexible IT staff augmentation. Pinnacle's core competencies include enterprise data warehousing and migration, custom application design and development, call center technology development and operations, systems and network installation, and IT-enabled vendor management solutions. Pinnacle serves a Fortune 500 client base on a nationwide basis via 19 service centers. Founded in 1996, Pinnacle has grown to become one of the largest and fastest growing Hispanic-owned and woman-owned companies in the United States.

Chapter Six

Kelly Lavorgna
MPL Systems, Inc.
www.mplsys.com

MPL Systems, Inc. (MPL) was founded in 1974 as a full-service telecommunications consulting firm. Today, MPL's scope of services includes: the provision of contract labor within information technology; help desk services; systems integration; systems management; infrastructure design/implementation; and equipment procurement. MPL has over 120 full-time technical consultants on assignment throughout the New York tri-state region and employs, on average, 30 part-time employees per week. In addition, MPL has numerous alliances with technology companies to enhance its service offerings.

Chapter Seven

Sue Romanos
CAREERXCHANGE
www.careerxchange.com

Since 1988, CAREERXCHANGE is one of south Florida's leading independent minority-owned and operated staffing companies, providing customized solutions to its customers to increase performance, reduce cycle times and improve return on investment through a contingent work force and placement of qualified full-time employees. CAREERXCHANGE distinguishes itself by providing a level of service to its clients above their expectations. Diversity.com has recently selected CAREERXCHANGE as a Top Diversity Owned Business, ranked #172 in the U.S. and #28 in Florida.

The company's principals have created an environment that acknowledges the challenges of balancing work and family life. The average tenure of a CAREERXCHANGE employee is 8.7 years, which translates into consistent quality service to its clients, year in and year out. Through an outside selection and survey process, CAREERXCHANGE has been chosen as a current finalist for the "Best Places to Work in South Florida" award by the *South Florida Business Journal.*

Annette Taddeo
LanguageSpeak
www.languagespeak.com

LanguageSpeak, Inc. is a full-service language company that provides document and web site translation, conference interpretation and on-site language instruction. Nationally certified by WBENC, NMSDC and the State of Florida, LanguageSpeak's services are available in over 100 languages, including Urdu, Mandarin Chinese and Farsi. LanguageSpeak has a network of over 300 professional translators, interpreters and instructors worldwide, who are all native speakers, certified and have a broad range of expertise and experience. Recognized by Forrester Research in its 2003 Minority Report as the foremost expert in the U.S. Hispanic Market, LanguageSpeak translated Office Depot's web site, the third largest ecommerce site on the web, into Spanish. LanguageSpeak was also recently recognized by the Small Business Administration as the Minority Small Business Champion of 2005.

Joe Tucker
Victory Personnel Services
www.victorypersonel.com

Victory Personnel is a full-service staffing agency with its headquarters in downtown Milwaukee. Victory has hundreds of contract employees working through out the United States in administrative, technical and professional positions for some of the country's most distinguished employers, such as Manpower, SBC, Miller Brewing Company, Abbott Labs, Motorola, Harley Davidson, Northwestern Mutual and IBM, just to name a few. Joe Tucker and Victory Personnel Services have received numerous awards and recognition, including: Entrepreneur of The Year 1992; Milwaukee Metropolitan Association of Commerce Future 50 list of fastest growing companies in 2000 and 2001; and Wisconsin Supplier Development Council's Supplier of the Year in 2002.

Chapter Nine

Joanne Harmelin
Harmelin Media
www.harmelin.com

Harmelin Media is a media buying service that plans and places all types of media including national and local TV, radio and cable, internet, newspapers and magazines. The company works with both consumer and business-to-business media. Harmelin also negotiates and plans sports media and sponsorships.